Screen Adaptation
Impure Cinema

DEBORAH CARTMELL AND
IMELDA WHELEHAN

palgrave
macmillan

First published 2010 by
PALGRAVE MACMILLAN

Palgrave Macmillan in the UK is an imprint of Macmillan Publishers Limited,
registered in England, company number 785998, of Houndmills, Basingstoke,
Hampshire RG21 6XS.

Palgrave Macmillan in the US is a division of St Martin's Press LLC,
175 Fifth Avenue, New York, NY 10010.

Palgrave Macmillan is the global academic imprint of the above companies
and has companies and representatives throughout the world.

Palgrave® and Macmillan® are registered trademarks in the United States,
the United Kingdom, Europe and other countries.

ISBN 978–1–4039–8549–1   hardback
ISBN 978–1–4039–8550–7   paperback

This book is printed on paper suitable for recycling and made from fully
managed and sustained forest sources. Logging, pulping and manufacturing
processes are expected to conform to the environmental regulations of the
country of origin.

A catalogue record for this book is available from the British Library.

A catalog record for this book is available from the Library of Congress.

10 9 8 7 6 5 4 3 2 1
19 18 17 16 15 14 13 12 11 10

Printed in China

To Hester Bradley, Jake Bradley, Laurence Sadler
and Miriam Sadler

Contents

Acknowledgements

Although we have been writing and teaching together in adaptation studies for over fifteen years, this is our first co-authored book on the subject. Many people have influenced the direction of our work over the ages, too many to name here, but here is a selection. Anne Beech of Pluto Press published the *Film/Fiction* annual in 1996 and we, with our co-editors I.Q. Hunter and Heidi Kaye, began our foray into an area that seemed to liberate us from the confines of literary studies whilst allowing us to ask new questions of old literary favourites.

Research for this book was facilitated, in part, by the British Academy. Some of the material included in Chapter 2 has developed from Deborah Cartmell, 'Film as the New Shakespeare and Film on Shakespeare: Reversing the Shakespeare/Film Trajectory', *Literature Compass* 3(5), 2006, 1150–9 and Chapter 5 from Deborah Cartmell and Imelda Whelehan, 'Harry Potter and the Fidelity Debate', in *Books in Motion: Adaptation, Intertextuality and Authorship*, ed. Mireia Aragay (Amsterdam and New York: Rodopi, 2005), pp. 37–50.

Our many students have provided some of the best and most provocative insights which we've carried forward and developed within our work. The Association of Adaptation Studies has brought us into direct communication with so many of the critics we admire and our journal *Adaptation* has allowed us privileged access to the newest work on adaptation today. Thanks to all. We're still enjoying ourselves.

Special thanks, as always, to David, Hester, Ian, Jake, Laurence and Miriam.

Introduction

In a collection published in 1936, Seymour Stem rants about the mechanical and infantilising process of screen adaptation in Hollywood: 'It means the reduction of every story to the lowest level of human intelligence, the assimilation of every idea to the spirit and grain of the universal Average Man.'[1] Advocates of adaptation studies have been contesting this view since the beginning of cinema, and only recently are there signs that the argument is beginning to be won. This volume attempts to pursue some of the reasons why literary adaptations on film and television have been so despised by critics; framing the subject is indeed difficult, but we've tried to strike a mean between a seemingly haphazard collection of case studies and a semi-deceitful promise that this volume offers a comprehensive, coherent and systematic overview of an area that just refuses to be pinned down.

Among the many dilemmas within the field is with what to call it. This book began with the working title of *Literature on Screen*, a logical extension of our recent collection of essays under that theme[2] and a testimony to the way our work has been nourished by the UK-based Association of Literature on Screen, established in 2006 and looking forward to its fifth annual conference in 2010. While the use of both 'literature' and 'screen' did, in our view, move us beyond the novel/film nexus to incorporate literature such as popular fiction, poetry, theatre, memoirs, and essays and screen to embrace television and video screens as well as films, 'adaptation' helpfully focuses on the process of exchange first and the concern with narrative form second. By popular consent in 2008 the Association of Literature on Screen became the Association of Adaptation Studies and with two eminent critics, Linda Hutcheon and Thomas Leitch, using the term 'adaptation' in their own recent monographs, perhaps the area is beginning to settle under a banner which can contain multitudes, and denies either 'literature' or 'film' unwelcome primacy. It would be impossible to do such a 'field' justice in a single book, and perhaps the time for attempting such a task is, thankfully, over. Instead, in this volume we are concerned with consolidating our own inquiries in the area, reflecting on the newest developments in the field and sharing some of our explorations and

1

interests, using a range of examples which, we hope, illustrate much wider points.

It is ten years since, in our 1999 publication *Adaptations: From Text to Screen, Screen to Text,* Imelda Whelehan attempted a critical over-view in 'Adaptation: The Contemporary Dilemmas';[3] in this volume we begin with a chapter which negotiates some of the issues crucial today, and mark out the changing boundaries of this constantly remapped critical terrain. The second chapter takes in the first half of the twenti-eth century in its historical sweep, reflecting on what filmmakers and film enthusiasts have to say about adaptations at a time when film was struggling to stake its own aesthetic claims. The third chapter looks at adaptations from a literary vantage and can be twinned with chapter 2 as it uncovers some of the reasons why it is not until around the turn of the last century that literature on screen begins to receive sustained critical attention and become a discipline in its own right. These two chapters also serve to lay out the key reasons why the development of adaptations studies as a critical approach which can make substantial theoretical challenges and contributions to contemporary film, media and literary scholarship has taken so long.

Champions of film, especially in the first half of the twentieth cen-tury, saw the adaptation as 'impure cinema' and resented the depend-ency of film on literature, especially during the period in which film was struggling to be regarded as an art form in its own right (or 'the new literature'). Such critics bear out Kamilla Elliott's claim that the war between literature and film springs from the desire for both to achieve 'purity' – film as the guardian of the image and novel as the guardian of the word.[4] Writers and literary critics considered film adaptations as abominations, crude usurpations of literary masterpieces that threat-ened both literacy and the book itself. Virginia Woolf, in her essay 'The Cinema', saw films as degrading, with readers being replaced with 'savages of the twentieth century watching the pictures';[5] similarly, the inaugural volume of *Scrutiny* (1932) included an essay on cinema by William Hunter entitled 'The Art-Form of Democracy?' in which he reflected on how films, in particular, narrative films, target the lowest possible denominator. Adaptations, especially, were regarded as 'the new opium', unworthy of mention in such a journal as *Scrutiny*, and were effectively banned from literary studies from 1932 onwards.[6]

Here the pervasive view of the cinema audience as hopelessly pas-sive and undiscriminating takes hold of high cultural criticism and so literary critics seek to reassure themselves that nothing can unseat literature. Needless to say, there were a number of film adaptations, as there are today, that were indeed poor and deserved the bad press, but actually most of these judgements appear to be constructed with little reference to any serious consideration of film. Moreover, most of the criticism, until the twenty-first century, was woefully predictable, judging an adaptation's merit by its closeness to its literary source or, even more vaguely, 'the spirit' of the book. Literature maintained its mystique as a solitary art unimpeded by the evils of commerce in such critical appraisal, even though this was a myth and enabled the perpetuation of the unexamined notion that money and art cannot mix. Furthermore, while adaptations were continually judged as effective or not, 'copies' of a transcendent original, they could only be a pale etiolated version of something distilled into a more 'palatable' form in face of the continued logocentric belief that words come first.[7] In this light adaptations can only be read as 'appropriation' and criticism has been bedevilled by emotive words such as 'violation', 'vulgarization' and 'betrayal', all emphasising what has been lost rather than what has been gained, and suggesting the forceful robbing of innocence from the pure literary text.

For many the study of adaptations has been restricted to a key focus on canonical texts, giving the screen adaptation a very difficult act to follow. Adaptations that have usurped their 'originals' in the minds of their audience – films like *The Wizard of Oz* (1939), *To Have and Have Not* (1944) or *Mary Poppins* (1964) – have failed to receive critical attention as adaptations. 'Bad adaptations' receive more coverage than 'good' ones, partly because they fulfil the prophecies of those who wish to see only artlessness in such a process and because there is little interest in the fate of the popular or middlebrow in writing on screen. Robert Stam identifies several sources of hostility to adaptation which he enumerates in the landmark essay which introduces the collection, *Literature and Film: A Guide to the Theory and Practice of Film Adaptation* (2005): the aesthetic prioritising of literature, the assumption (which has to some extent become a reality in critical approaches to adaptation) that there is a rivalry between literature and film, the prejudice against the 'embodiedness' of the visual image, the uncontested belief in the value of words, 'the myth of facility' (the conviction that films are easy to make and watch), accompanied by class prejudice, that film appeals to the masses rather than to a cultured elite (and that this is a bad thing), and a conviction that adaptations immorally live off and drain 'the spirit' of their literary sources.[8] To varying extents, these mindsets dogged adaptation studies over the last century, and in failing to cast all or some of these largely unacknowledged prejudices off, adaptations scholars were in many cases their own worst enemies.

The latter part of the book considers selected adaptations through the contexts of authorship (Chapter 4), appropriation (Chapter 4), reception (Chapter 5), intertextuality (Chapter 5), genrification, genre (Chapters 6 and 7) and the phenomenon of the multiple adaptation (Chapter 8), where a number of films return to the same text to 'violate' it repeatedly with some striking accumulative effects. Although it is tempting to boast that this book can offer an 'overview', this would be overambitious, not to say impossible to achieve. Fortunately the time has passed when one critic can possess the subject knowledge to claim the power of overview: while our strengths in literary and film studies are complemented by our interest in the cultural industries, the law, video game technology and new media, we would not pretend to be able to intervene in these growth areas in any profound or sustained way at present. If anything, this book is our acknowledgement that the field of adaptations extends beyond our current scope; long may it continue to extend and confound our expectations, challenging the comforts of disciplinary integrity.

We have had the privilege of working and publishing in the field of adaptations studies since the mid-1990s and of sharing with and profiting from the ideas, perspectives and positions put forward by an increasingly formidable group of adaptation theoreticians. A number of these same writers have been responsible for landmark shifts in the available responses to adaptations. Brian McFarlane's reading of adaptations through a narratological framework exhorted readers to examine and codify the narrative strategies of literature on screen – a fine antidote to the strategy of bemoaning what's missing from a film of a book. McFarlane's engagement with narrative voice and its filmic replacement (the camera eye for the 'I') and the ways in which voice is translated into extra-cinematic codes has been taken on board by a number of scholars, most notably Robert Stam who, introducing his co-edited collection, *Literature and Film* (2005, with Alessandra Raengo), reiterates the significance of narratology for 'analysing certain formal aspects of film adaptations'[9] even while he emphasises the additional importance of context, whether that be historical, social or academic.

A variety of approaches can be utilised when reflecting on different adaptations of a single literary text; here we've chosen adaptations of Louisa May Alcott's nineteenth-century novels, *Little Women* and *Good Wives*. McFarlane's deployment of narratological codes, of course, in common with Barthes's undertaking in *S/Z* (1970) extends from the formal to the contextual, and this can be demonstrated under the category of 'visual codes' by looking at the opening credits of the 1933 film of *Little Women* which are seen against a painting of the author, Louisa May Alcott's own home, Orchard House, in a snowy landscape framed by trees, with a woman in the left-hand corner, seen from behind, approaching the door. The effect is to draw you into the warmth of the home, symbolic of family and comfort. This is taken a stage further in the opening credits of the 1949 film which are set against an embroidered picture of the four girls in a snowy landscape, which gives place to an embroidery of the Alcott homestead with a figure seen from behind, pulling a Christmas tree. Again, the picture visually draws you in and signifies domestic comforts, Christmas pleasures and family values. In the 1994 film, the *mise-en-scène* of the opening shots presents us with a sequence of traditional Christmas-card pictures: a town covered in snow, a wreath being placed on a door, the replica Orchard House in winter with a well-wrapped woman approaching, a horse-drawn carriage, a wooden fence covered in snow, and a huge Christmas tree being dragged through a snowy lane. The familiar images of 'traditional Christmases' visually guarantee the film to be heart-warming and family-centred and this example also serves to show how both subsequent film adaptations adopt similar iconography to establish the same opening mood in audiences spanning six decades.

Another way to look at the three films is in their relationship to the source text by adopting taxonomical readings. There are numerous attempts to categorize 'types' of adaptations; to name one of the least complicated, Geoffrey Wagner suggests dividing adaptations into three:

1. transposition – in which the screen version sticks closely to the literary source, with a minimum of interference
2. commentary – where the original is purposely or unwittingly altered due to the intentions of the film-maker
3. analogy – a completely different work of art which is a substantial departure from the original.[10]

In spite of 'liberties' taken with the novels *Little Women* and *Good Wives,* the 1933 film directed by George Cukor and the 1949 adaptation directed by Mervyn LeRoy (very similar in structure due to the fact that two of the same screenwriters were used) are what Wagner identifies as 'transpositions' of the text; while increasingly diminishing the Christian context, the family values and the relationship of the sisters are very close to Alcott's two novels. The 1994 adaptation, with Susan Sarandon and Winona Ryder, can be regarded as a 'commentary' akin to a critical reading of the film privileging feminism; Gillian Armstrong's film uses Susan Sarandon (with film baggage from the likes of *The Witches of Eastwick,* 1987 and *Thelma and Louise,* 1991) to inject an overtly pro-feminist perspective on Alcott's narrative by allowing Marmie to speak out against the restrictions of women's clothing and to encourage (rather than discourage, as in the text), the ambitions of her daughters. Going further afield, you can see traces of *Little Women* in other TV sitcoms and films, which can be regarded as loose 'analogies', such as Woody Allen's *Hannah and her Sisters* (1986), which moves the focus of the story from Jo to Laurie (Allen). Using taxonomies to suggest degrees of separation between 'original' text and adaptation is as old as the field itself, of course, and categories have multiplied and diversified to the extent that in Kamilla Elliott's *Rethinking the Novel/Film Debate* (2003) there are six approaches in evidence. The danger of posing such a model of approach is whether such taxonomies risk privileging the notion of 'closeness to origin' as the key business of adaptation studies; additionally the boundaries between the various classifications are impossible to define and an adaptation can fit into a number of categories at once. Yet the will to taxonomise is a distinctive feature of adaptation studies, which reflects more than anything its need to establish a critical perspective of its own.

Considering the films in relation to reception arguably produces more useful results and allows us to focus on the process of adaptation as a business proposition where 'property' has a clear purpose in the market place. We need to ask the question: why make a film of *Little Women* in 1933, 1949 and 1994? What do the films tell us about the period in which they are based? How do they appropriate the novels for their own political, social and economic purposes? The approach adopted here owes much to Cultural Materialist criticism, which emerged in Shakespeare and Renaissance studies in the 1980s. As John Brannigan has explained, while opposing formalist readings that divorced literature from history, cultural materialists 'scrutinized how literary texts played their part in sustaining and perpetuating conservative ideologies'.[11] Their interest is in both the text and its afterlife (possibly all a text has) and looking at how a text has been constructed for a particular audience is especially illuminating when there are several versions of a single narrative. At a glance, the 1933 film, starring

Katherine Hepburn, begins with Marmie at work in a wartime refuge, offering money to a poor father who has stoically endured family losses in the Civil War. Shortages of food and clothing here surely reference the audience's own situation during the Great Depression. Made between the wars, the film doesn't shy away from its political context, whereas in 1949, there's virtually no mention of the war, and Beth's death is neither shown nor explicitly reported. The 'poverty' of the March family is ignored in this adaptation that features extravagant costumes and plush interiors of the family home. Post-war, the production valorises domesticity, minimalises the emotional effects of the loss of a child, and showcases prosperity.

In recent years it has become common practice to start from the assumption that all adaptations have more than a single source and consider how an understanding of intertextuality or what Gérard Genette, in *Palimpsestes* (1982), calls transtextuality, opens up the study of literature on screen to allow further contextual readings.[12] Taking Genette's 'intertextuality' (quotation or allusion to something else), it is obvious how the 1994 adaptation of *Little Women* pays homage to and borrows from the earlier films, especially in the use of Orchard House. Another example is in the closing frames of Mervyn LeRoy's 1949 film with the couple returning to the house framed by a rainbow – an intertextual reference to LeRoy's earlier film, *The Wizard of Oz* (1939).[13]

Finally, we approach literature on screen via genre. In all three films, the narrative has been rewritten to allow the heroine to have both the (increasingly attractive) husband and a promising career as a writer, whereas Alcott's book forces Jo to make a choice: not a nice ending for Hollywood. In the novel, or at least in the penultimate chapter of *Good Wives,* the point at which all three films choose to end, the compression of 'true love' and 'authorship' is incrementally manufactured: in 1933, a rather decrepit Professor Bhaer (played by an old-looking 38-year-old Paul Lukas) proposes to Jo while surprising her with her (unnamed) book, fresh from the printers; in 1949, a much more dapper and younger-looking Professor (played by 33-year-old Rossano Brazzi) issues her with a volume entitled *My Beth;* while in 1994 the sexiest of all professors (44-year-old Gabriel Byrne) is chased by Jo after she receives from him proofs of the novel entitled *Little Women.* As we move forward in time, the films become more 'genrified' in the restructuring of the narrative in terms of the narrative strategies of romance and biopic. The latter can be seen in the explicit identification invoked between Jo and Louisa May Alcott (who emphatically regarded professional authorship and matrimony as incompatible), with the last film commencing with the voice-over narration of Jo, the author of her own story.

Thomas Leitch has proposed considering adaptation (in particular, those that self-consciously position themselves as adaptations) as a genre in its own right[14] and, in a sense, any attempt to arrive at a systematic overview, like genre criticism, imposes one's own critical construct onto screen adaptation based on a culturally determined reading of its distinctive features. For a good part of a century, adaptations, while popular at the box office, have been, for literary and film critics, among the most despised forms of entertainment, often referred to as 'mixed cinema' or even more damning, 'impure' film, implying that film and literature when combined are mutually contaminating or polluting of each other. Mindful of such charges and of the impossibility of both recovering an adaptation and divorcing it from our own concerns, this book attempts to offer approaches that reverse the tendency to covertly belittle the adaptation as evidence of the cultural decline of the society in which it was produced while resisting the temptation to draw boundaries or to enforce single and reductive readings onto a field which seems to defy such containment. In the past the pursuit for purity in these two narrative forms has inhibited the growth of a more interdisciplinary celebration of the cross-fertilisations between literature and film and only adaptations theorists seem comfortable with the fact that adaptation is at the centre of the development of commercial fiction film. For some the field of adaptation studies remains too literary-focused and for others it gives unwarranted precedence to inferior films. There has been an over-entrenched concern with the differing 'industry conditions' of literature versus film and an uninterrogated assumption that we still read in the same way even while our viewing habits have changed demonstrably. Maybe it is stating the obvious, but commercial film and the numerous ways we can choose to watch it in the wake of DVD and digital technologies make it as portable and flexible as a novel; moreover, despite the admiration for literary stylistics and postmodern experimentation, people devour adaptations of realist representational novels as much as they always have.

With this in mind we offer this book as another contribution to the cluster of positions on adaptation. The book aims to offer a debate to be continued with some of the most interesting critics in the field and, more than this, attempts to provide the reader with a guide to the field itself and the subtle inflections that have marked a near-paradigm shift in the last decade, as well as some of key positions and perspectives offered by critics since the dawning of cinema and well before the 'field' of adaptations studies had any meaning. The aim, as always, is to offer insights and debates useful to those with little knowledge in the area as much as it is directed to our colleagues whose own work, taken as a whole, reflects our increasing confidence in the space we occupy across the disciplines of literary, film and TV studies, and beyond.

1

Adaptations: Theories, Interpretations and New Dilemmas

Nearly a decade ago, we characterised the area of adaptations studies as still 'caught between literary criticism and film studies'.[1] One sea change, as we examine today's dilemmas for adaptation studies, is that discussions about where to situate the study of adaptations recede and other questions are posed from different perspectives. Linda Hutcheon brings to adaptations her abiding interest in intertextuality, and in her 2006 book she focuses on 'modes of engagement – telling, showing, and interacting with stories',[2] also emphasising that 'the contexts of creation and reception are material, public, and economic as much as they are cultural, personal, and aesthetic'.[3] In this way she displaces her own putative disciplinary location and skirts round the issue of medium specificity, not to ignore the formal qualities of the medium but in order to emphasise the social and cultural processes of exchange in adaptation.

Since the late 1990s, there has been a tendency among scholars of screen adaptation to announce their own perspectives on the field as some kind of corrective to what has gone before. In order to emphasise what is new, challenging and refreshing, it has been felt necessary to debunk older theories, adjust the partial visions (as they are seen) offered by others and propose new modes of perception. The impetus of this is apparent – though many will return to George Bluestone's *Novels into Film* (1957) to suggest the longevity of some ideas – the field is young and has, relatively speaking, suddenly become crowded with a heady mix of critical voices who all do indeed have something new to offer. But maybe the correctives have gone as far as they can for the time being; maybe it would be useful to declare a moratorium on some features of key debates, or curb the will to taxonomise just for long enough to observe what taxonomies give us. Possibly one of the most audacious 'correctives' published recently is *From Camera Lens to Critical Lens*, edited by Rebecca Housel, which is subtitled 'A Collection of Best Essays on Film Adaptation' and in whose introduction it uncompronisingly states, 'Film adaptation is a vehicle for life experiences.'[4] This anthology seems surprisingly unaware of most of the critical work done in the field and is one example of a small body of work moving against the main tide of theory, or at least an example of an attitude to adaptations that refuses to go away.

As with any lively and meaningful area of academic study there *are* necessary correctives to make; and the field itself is changing rapidly to the point that some areas of primary concern here would have not had currency in Bluestone's time, nor would they be considered when Wagner was writing or even when McFarlane, in the mid-1990s, refocused our attention back towards narrative. Thomas Leitch is clear that there is such a thing as adaptation *theory*, that it has been in existence since George Bluestone's *Novels into Film*, and that the study of adaptations directly contributed to the emergence of film studies in the academy. The earliest films studied in the academic environment in American institutions were, he argues, 'adaptations of canonical classics that served as adjuncts to the literary canon and classic works of cinema that could be studied as members of a quasi-literary cinematic canon'.[5] In this light the 'literary' provenance of adaptations studies is a given, something that excites and repels critics (depending usually on their critical location) in equal measure. What is more interesting is the way in which Leitch distinguishes between 'the theory and practice of adaptation studies'[6] and the growing disjunction between the two, where the former concerns itself with developing a body of knowledge which formalises perspectives taken as understandings of the subject itself, and the latter continues to compare and contrast literary texts and films or, to a lesser degree, television, with particular reference to authorial intentions and literary conventions of study.

Christine Geraghty's recent foray into this debate begins with a refusal to itemise the development of adaptation studies since Bluestone or to engage with modes of discourse that conclude ultimately with a version of the 'it wasn't like that in the book' statement. Geraghty rightly notes that 'it is time to move on'[7] and this is a view shared widely (except for Housel et al.) amongst the most influential writers on adaptations of our day. Geraghty resists what she perceives to be a continuing and dominant literary tendency in studies in adaptation; in an attempt to decouple the adapting text from the notion of a single source she announces her intention to focus on the 'films themselves and the work of "recall"'[8] so that what is looked for are references to the adaptive status of the film within its own terms. Geraghty isn't alone in this wish to decouple the literary text from the adapted medium, and her work chimes with and develops many of the theoretical and critical statements issued in the last decade. Her focus on the concern with space and landscape reminds us that contemporary adaptation critics more often concern themselves with the discourses surrounding the text as much as the formal qualities of the text itself, in a pronounced shift from the critical practices adopted so impressively by McFarlane.

We share Geraghty's frustration with the tendency to foreground the literary in a nod to its still privileged cultural status; but we wonder whether focusing on the 'films themselves' is possible or desirable when studying the process of adaptation. One of the seductions of adaptation criticism is that the literary text will not disappear, and its traces (often obscured or unacknowledged) come to the surface in numerous ways, just as an adaptation, particularly a successful one, inhabits and imprints itself upon the notional 'original'. The more one follows the traces of adapted texts, the more one follows paths beyond the literary, the cinematic or the televisual (as Geraghty, Leitch, Hutcheon and Elliott demonstrate in their re-evaluations of the field). Naturally the further one moves from locating the heart of adaptation studies as residing on the literary/screen nexus, the more boundless and indefinable the area becomes.

It is ironic, therefore, that the further adaptation moves from locatability in either or any discipline, the more definable we want it to be. In the past decade we have truly entered the era of definitions and boundary marking, which offers us a distinctive cluster of theories of adaptation, which mark themselves as discrete from anthologies and case studies, which are identified as 'practice'. Perhaps, therefore, it is worthwhile to pause here a moment and reflect on what constitutes the academic study of adaptation. Can we now assert that it is itself an area of study which is inter- or perhaps trans-disciplinary, rather than a 'tendency' locatable from a number of disciplinary perspectives? Even now and in spite of what are overgeneralised as 'poststructuralist' approaches to adaptation,[9] regarded as having marginalised or theorised the concerns of fidelity-seekers in adaptation, the study of adaptations can still bring out the nascent prejudices in the most acute critic.

Despite the 'theory wars', the maturing of film studies and the flourishing of cultural studies, literature is seen to have a higher moral calling than its younger, and some have argued, lesser sibling. Other Media and Cultural studies commentators' concerns with film and literature spinoffs, in video games, mash-ups and 'fan fic' might find their territory invaded by those in adaptation studies who are specifically interested in cultural products which contain further evidence of the will to adapt, recycle and appropriate. Adaptation is an area of cross-fertilisation best summed up by Robert Stam's critical approach, which rejects 'the standard rhetoric [which] has often deployed an elegiac discourse of loss, lamenting what has been "lost" in the transition from novel to film, while ignoring what has been "gained".'[10] He talks in terms of fertilisation and exchange: 'Adaptations redistribute energies and intensities, provoke flows and displacements; the linguistic energy of literary writing turns into the audio-visual-kinetic-performative energy of the adaptation, in an amorous exchange of textual fluids.'[11]

Despite Stam's revisioning of what is normally regarded as contaminations of the energy supplied by adaptation, there is still a trace of yearning, of a desire for simplicity and disciplinary purity at a time when interdisciplinary ventures are yielding some challenging insights. Adaptations seem to evoke particular ire among some such 'purists', in whatever discipline or sub-area they are found – rather flatteringly, it is as if there is some tangible fear that adaptation studies' existence detracts in some way from the other disciplinary integrity, or other 'hybrid' adventures in cultural studies. For all these sometimes heated debates, the fields of Film, Television and Literary studies have always had much to gain from each other. If one were to attempt to express the relationships between literature, film and written text to screen adaptations in the form of a Venn diagram it might appear thus:

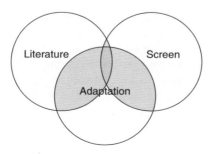

As narrative forms, literature and screen have historically enriched each other. There is no term to use that doesn't imply a partial vision to someone, or which doesn't confuse the two forms. To use 'text' as if one is referring to a written form of narrative is to ignore the status of film as text; to use 'novel' is to ignore poetry, drama, biography, the essay – all fruitful sources for adaptation. Literature embraces all these things, and expressed in lower case, it should not be taken to imply canonical status. The term 'screen' is again not the happiest choice for everyone. It is used so as to be as all-embracing as possible – it covers the cinema screen, the TV screen and the computer screen where video games might be played, DVDs viewed, digital TV content downloaded or internet sites accessed. Many commentators have already noted how, during the modernist period, 'literary writers' were fascinated by how the textual possibilities of film might enrich their own narrative strategies; filmmakers, in their developing art over the twentieth century, showed how the medium might offer the psychological and symbolic depths latterly felt to only be the province of the 'high' arts. We have depicted the overlap between the two to be slight because there is also an opposing force pulling them apart, comprising issues such as the will to disciplinary purity on the part of some scholars, the need for film to be sometimes independent of adapted literature in the market-place in order to raise enough income to sustain future productions. The field of adapations, however, derives substantial impetus and philosophical nourishment from both areas; but there is also a significant part of it that is original and independent of these areas. Our claim here, symbolised by the diagram above, is that studying adaptations produces something new that neither belongs to film nor literature; it may well continue the legacy of theoretical debates touching narratology, spectatorship, the arts economy, and so on, but the material is entirely a consequence of the choice to accept that adaptation is a process which *is of scholarly interest in its own right*.

For those who accept this formulation and think in fact that this much is understood, we offer another representation which attempts to visualise and summarise the state of adaptations today, beyond concern with disciplines and purely extracting approaches which may be common or applicable to several subject areas. Here the putative 'field' of adaptations studies is surrounded or shaped by the dominant discourses of textual enquiry which circulate in its wake. Rather than being framed as indebted (or profoundly prejudiced) by one topic over

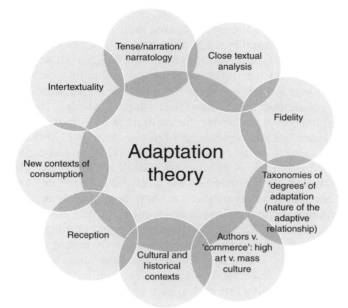

another, adaptation studies is as much a creation of these discourses as well as sustaining them by its existence.

Adaptations themselves absorb and bounce back to us the debates and observations we make about them – since there is now an interest in adaptations *as* adaptations, in scholarly domains, the broadsheets (think of the UK *Guardian*'s recent 'Adaptation of the week' series and UK Film4's Great Adaptations season 2009), and in the marketing and reviewing of films. It is inevitable that the market adjusts to provide for our needs and to capitalise on our pleasures, and both *Adaptation* (Jonze, 2002) and *A Cock and Bull Story* (Winterbottom, 2005) are contemporary examples of this phenomenon. The selection of seemingly 'unfilmable' texts allows both films to produce a commentary on the impossibility or perhaps the undesirability of faithful or authentic adaptation. *Adaptation*'s narrative focus becomes the scriptwriter's struggle to offer a faithful rendition of Susan Orlean's *The Orchid Thief* (1998). The embattled 'serious' screenwriter is haunted by the easy embracing of genre of his twin brother: as he tries to break his writer's block by listening to the screenwriting guru

Robert McKee, the movie proceeds to unravel every central edict of the craft and exposes the screenwriting industry as itself inflected by norms in taste, themselves made to be broken. *A Cock and Bull Story* dramatises some of the absurdities about the baggage attached to classic adaptation and the quest for historical authenticity in the scene where an historical adviser is portrayed as having an anorakish concern with contemporary costume and weapons which is clearly demonstrated to be over and above the needs of 'story' – more so since the novel adapted is Laurence Sterne's *Tristram Shandy* (1759), the most notorious shaggy-dog story in literary history. Their respective commentaries on the process of adaptation itself are interwoven into the film's narration, so that they become a central feature and can nearly silence our will to analyse them, as they have already analysed the field and their very conditions of production, for us.

If adaptations are themselves doing the work of adaptation criticism for us, we adaptations scholars might fairly regard ourselves as running to keep up with a field which is fast developing with evey new critical 'corrective' offered, with every new taxonomy presented complete with innumerable theoretical pegs upon which to hang our criticisms. We may feel the need to choose from many possibilities offered by these changes – some ideological, some methodological and some technological – as competently as we can, without the previous anxieties about the disciplinary spectres which may or may not haunt us.

The term 'adaptation' suggests the possibilities of ranging far beyond the domains of literature on screen; other terms which come into play are intertextuality (a contested term in its possible scope and suggestion of freeplay) and hypertextuality (which allows consideration of all texts superimposed upon an earlier one – including imitation, pastiche, parody and adaptation). Obviously Gérard Genette's exhaustive study of 'hypertextuality' in *Palimpsests* (1982) offers another way in which one might begin to characterise the nature of the relationship between hyper- and hypo-text beyond that of parody, pastiche, expansion, and so forth, ad nauseam. What is always appealing about Genette's work is that he recognises the extent to which his taxonomies depend upon the accident of the texts he knows well; in this he gives licence for all of us to recognise that taxonomies are only useful in helping to explicate the theoretical positioning of one person and also, by arbitrarily positioning texts according to preordained categories, allowing new insights and unexpected connections to flow through these novels. The ambitions of film adaptations are not always motivated by the text but rather by the paratext(s), one of which is the economic potential in producing a hypertext which both supplants and returns readers to the hypotext.

The recognition of the arbitrariness of the nomenclature surrounding adaptations might also allow some new inteventions into the politics of the 'case-study' approach to adaptation criticism, taking us beyond the deadlock identified by Robert B. Ray in his highly influential piece 'Literature and Film'[12] and reiterated in Geraghty's 2008 book. Clearly if a 'case study' amounts to an attempt at like-for-like comparison between 'source' and adaptation, such an account has little relevance to the wider study of adaptations as a *process*. Yet in more complex ways, as advocates of an intertextual or dialogic approach suggest, each relationship between texts is individualised and dependent upon the fate of those two (or more) texts and what results by their interconnection and cross-referencing. Added to that layer of meaning is the number of approaches which one can take in relation to that connection, process or relationship, whether it be via genre, historical location, star identities, authorship, music, or some combination of several of these perspectives. As Geraghty notes: 'Familiar stories and generic references fold into one another; one setting can be seen through another, and characters are created from the ghosts of actors who have played them.'[13] While some critics are primarily concerned only with adapations which announce themselves as such, it is clear that different kinds of adaptations encourage us to focus on different areas of interest and others operate on givens that are worth foregrounding, and provide the focus of our critical attention. For instance, some aspects of well-known books have always already been encountered by the potential film audience regardless of whether they've read the book – and it is these aspects that can be considered as most crucial. If one was going to group texts this way, one would end up with some interesting categories, where Mr Darcy from *Pride and Prejudice* would happily coexist with both Scrooge from *A Christmas Carol* and James Bond from Fleming's series of novels (see Bennett and Woollacott's pathfinding *Bond and Beyond*, 1987), and with historical personages whose iconography precedes any 'real' historical account of them – for example, Elizabeth I or Napoleon.

Our readings of texts in this volume do not purport to offer definitive accounts in and of themselves, or of the exchange between a text and its adaptation. We agree with Jonathan Gray that 'both reading and the text are a continual jouney *through*, a continuance of motion, and while there might be determinate moments, there are always potentially more determinate moments to come'.[14] We may review the literary text in light of the screened version or alternatively find ourselves mentally returning and reinterpeting the film as a result of new or first readings of the literary text. We retain the practice of looking at 'case studies', but hope in doing so that we problematise what has been seen as its compare-and-contrast simplicity, because of our belief that each adaptive process generates its own nexus of relations and that the pleasure of studying adaptations is in part one of discovery and of the creative aspect of putting several textual readings together in a new constellation.

We have from early on in our involvement in the field been fascinated and challenged by the difference a consideration of popular texts and genre makes to the framework of adaptation studies.[15] It's important to note that what is most significant about studying genre is its fluidity and its status as a cultural category as well as descriptor – itself not fixed, but in some ways a short cut to defining (and meeting) audience expectations: 'Each new text we encounter carries with it the potential to expand, or otherwise modify, our knowledge of its genre's semantics and syntax.'[16] As Gray points out, when we have an intimate knowledge of a genre we enter a 'discursive cluster' which confers a group or community identity, and which needs to be taking into account our awareness of how we engage with genre texts and how such engagement can be a cumulative exercise, depending upon the depth or breadth of our knowledge of such a genre.

Just as a decade ago it was essential to quote Joseph Conrad and D.W. Griffith at the start of any critique of adaptation, it is now *de rigueur* to posit the question, 'When is an "adaptation" not an adaptation?', even if one does not answer it. Thanks to the writings of Hutcheon and Stam and with a nod to narratology and particularly Gérard Genette, we ponder the question, when do we move into intertextuality and paratextuality? In common with Linda Hutcheon we would not count allusion, quotation or other brief acquaintances with a text as 'adaptation', but rather as a condition of our cultural embracing of intertexuality or the 'postmodern' condition of quoting and alluding; but adaptation for us must posit a more influential relationship than this. It is not that we demand adaptations acknowledge their status as such, but that it is a sustained recognition where the adaptation utilises the text it appropriates or adapts with a purpose, even if that purpose isn't explicitly announced; alternatively, we are also fascinated by the act of discovering a text which seems to owe part of its impetus to an unacknowledged source – it is a 'found adaptation' such as seems to be the case in recent interest in Don Quixote as a source text for Pixar's *Toy Story*.[17]

What is significant in such exchanges in a 'found' or unannounced adaptive relationship is often in the space in between, the paratexts are all those objects and signs that mediate the relationships between text and reader. Genette's rule of thumb to test the significance of the paratext in interpretation is this: 'To indicate what is at stake, we can ask one simple question as an example: limited to the text alone and without a guiding set of directions, how would we read Joyce's *Ulysses* if it were not entitled *Ulysses*?'[18] Genette, always fond of taxonomising, constantly breaks down his categories into sub-sections, but helpfully provides a basic formula which helps to distinguish the paratexts that come materially with the text and those which are spatially separate in some way : 'for those who are keen on formulae, *paratext = peritext + epitext*',[19] with the epitext being that not materially appended to the text, unlike blurbs, reviewer's quotations, and so forth, and presumably including critical essays and adaptations which recall the text in the mind of the consumer. Obviously printed epitexts can become part of the peritext subsequently, such as scholarly introductions: but all the paratexts Genette cites tend to refer to that material produced by author, publisher, reviewer or another writer about this writer. We wonder how he would characterise the kind of pre-release publicity that sets up expectations and delineates reader/viewerships and that is in essence built out of 'nothing', or certainly in another way has nothing to do with the text – for example the high-profile press coverage of Renée Zellweger's weight gain undertaken to play Bridget in the film *Bridget Jones's Diary* (2001), or the constant pronouncements about the cultishness of Richard Yates's *Revolutionary Road* (1961) before the release of Mendes's 2008 film. 'Star discourse' is another increasingly popular mode of intervention into adaptation in recognition that stars affect the circulation of film properties as much when adaptations are made as when they fail to be made,[20] and reading the adaptation through the other performances of a star or stars generates new possibilities in adaptation studies, just as reading through costume or soundtrack uncovers new connections and hidden legacies.

Although we talk about adaptation criticism as if its critical role is its first principle, in fact a number of books which talk of fiction and film are notably *un*critical, their prime concern being that of establishing which screened version of a well-known novel (the prime focus of collections even today) is the best. The reasons are left as self-evident – the legacy of the past follies of fidelity criticism and the overweening

assumption that analysts of novels can swiftly and effortlessly turn
their attentions to film versions, deploying the same kind of thematic
analysis that they use in their approach to fiction still has currency
in some recent work, so that for many it is the trademark adaptation
'style'. E. Ann Kaplan speculates that

> the haste to make the great realist novel into film and television versions
> has to do with a cultural anxiety about the continuity of both genres – realist
> fiction and illusionist film – in an era of rapidly developing digital technol-
> ogies, such as websites, internet, virtual reality and CD-ROM technologies.
> All these raise questions about the future of film and canonical fiction.[21]

It may be that this is a partial explanation of the 1990s craze for classic
adaptation; it allows us to focus on films which we might see as doing
interesting things with books, but is itself a prematurely tired old form
whose continuity is being challenged by the episodic and intermittent
pleasures of the internet and the mash-up.

We want to break ranks a little here in refusing to *not* discuss fidelity, even though we agree with Dudley Andrew's judgement, made
back in 1980, that it is 'the most frequent and most tiresome discussion of adaptation ... Here it is assumed that the task of adaptation
is the reproduction in cinema of something essential about an original text; we have a clear-cut case of a film trying to measure up to a
literary work, or of an audience expecting to make such a comparison'.[22] Fidelity is tiresome as a critical strategy not least because it is
an inexact science deployed to compare often something as inchoate
as the 'spirit' of the thing; but the desire for it or the dread of it haunts
many a film spectator's imagination and the intent lurks behind many
a screenwriter's claim to get to the heart of the source text. In a recent
collection, Robin Swicord (author of adaptations ranging from *Little
Women*, 1994, to *The Curious Case of Benjamin Button*, 2008) even
talks about 'getting down to the DNA'[23] of a novel, tantalisingly implying that faithful exchange is possible if only we can drill down to the
smallest of components of the narrative in question; that a matter
of scientifically executed dissection might yield the best results. We
know what she is really saying here and in some ways it is hard not
to be sympathetic: many screenwriters are often charged with the job
of realising a well-known text on screen and their duty is to show an
understanding of it in all its complexity, and to distil what Barthes
would call its 'cardinal functions' whilst losing none of its flavour or
the reasons for its popularity with readers. Fidelity remains at the
fringes of the study of adaptations, but it dominates popular reviews

and fan sites alike. Andrew is right in seeing it as one of the dullest of strands in adaptation criticism generally speaking: but at times it is at the heart of an adaptation event, such as the first three Harry Potter films. At those times the fact of 'fidelity' is a useful theme of discussion, particularly in contrast to the later more 'cinematic' offerings. For the editors of one recent collection, 'fidelity persists as a value despite the post-structuralist onslaught',[24] and they make the case for plurality in the wake of what they see as the multiplying discourses of adaptation stretching to infinity. In his oft-quoted essay, Andrew also talks about the need for adaptation to take a 'sociological turn' which directs focus on to the possibilities of repurposing for a new audience in a different time or cultural context, foregrounding its dependency on 'the complex interchange among eras, styles, nations, and subjects'.[25] Contemporary commentators, especially Geraghty, but also Murray, have taken up this call and in fact rather than turn to close film analysis as an antidote to the 'literary' features of classic adaptation criticism, the turn has been to the social, historical, economic and contextual criticism in a cross-disciplinary blending, which smacks of what Lévi-Strauss would call *bricolage*.

For many the anxiety of not being able to pin down the activities of adaptation studies, or indeed the categories of adaptations we find on further investigation, remains. The number of categories has mutated from three broad groupings (for example transposition, commentary, analogy in Wagner's terminology[26]) ranging from one extreme to the other, to a multitude of variations. In terms of defining what we *do* when we 'do' adaptation, it's often easier to try to identify what we don't or 'shouldn't' do, as does Thomas Leitch in his article, 'Twelve Fallacies in Adaptation Theory'.[27] Whether the debate is about what we do, what we shouldn't do, or how to compare the adaptation that shifts historical context and adds a post- colonial reading to that which positions itself as homage, we seem to want the ground laid out before us, so that each taxonomy designates a clearly signposted avenue. Of course in the attempt to anticipate every possible permutation of the relationship between one narrative form and another we attempt a list that will never be exhaustive but is, frankly, exhausting and does not produce the holy grail of the definitive critical model which helps us further analyse the process of adaptation. Necessarily these taxonomies display the prejudices and partialities of their inventor (and Genette and Elliott, to name but two, are candid about this) and are themselves most often adaptations of the taxonomies laid out previously by another commentator.

We are going to eschew the very real temptation to taxonomise in this volume in order to return to the most simple of motivations: what fascinates us about adaptation is the process and the relationships assumed or unannounced between one literary text and the creators of a screen text. There are other narrative adaptive relationships, assuredly, some of which, like the relationship between novel and drama, have had some serious attention in the past; there are others which announce the changing framework of new media. But for us what is compelling about the literature/screen nexus is that the relationship is as old as the development of narrative cinema and it summons up questions of authority (literally as author or re-creator), economy, rights, ideology and audience engagement, at the same time as the history of adaptation criticism in the borders of film and literary studies is testament to the conflicting agenda of critical and theoretical priorities in both. For us it is the excitement of encountering in every site of adaptation an entirely new set of relations which allows us to draw promiscuously on theoretical tendencies in film and literary studies and to observe how, in that process of adaptation, something unique is produced.

For this and so many reasons by now obvious to the reader, this book cannot hope to and does not want to pretend to have the last word about adaptation. In restricting our purview largely to the fields of 'literature' and 'screen' (partly because of our own current academic strengths, partly for preference) we still have vast critical expanses before us, some of which will remain uncharted territory in this instance. The textual examples we dwell on are not there as 'case studies' if by that the reader takes something pejorative (following on from Robert B. Ray's provocatively argued essay), but offer moments when adaptive exchange tells us something interesting about any of the issues set out above. There is a vast amount of subjectivity and contingency involved in this, just as some of the examples deployed display the 'anxiety of influence' typical of most critical work in the Humanities where we remain mindful of what has gone before and, good *bricoleurs* that we are, repurpose perspectives and strategies that have served other critics well in quite other environments. The old faithfuls appear because classic literary texts have been the bulwark of adaptation studies since the late 1950s and continue to be a particularly buoyant niche area of the film and TV industries; other examples emerge from our experience as teachers of adaptation; others are necessarily even more arbitrary, chance discoveries.

Also of concern here are the changing historical responses to adaptation in the film industry itself where literary properties have been the staple of filmmaking practice; yet how much one wants to make that relationship explicit in the marketing of a particular film can vary enormously. When we reflect back to the period of classic Hollywood we see that at the same time as well-known literary classics are being reproduced and announced as such, bestselling authors of the day are finding their novels 'optioned' (before publication in some cases), and the resulting film may only lag behind the published text by one or two years. Such writers – the Booth Tarkingtons, James Hiltons and Olive Higgins Proutys of this world – have faded from the notice of literary scholars, even of popular fiction, and their work remains most palpable in the classic films which resulted (*The Magnificent Ambersons, Random Harvest, Stella Dallas*, and so forth). For many, these classic Hollywood movies will be the first acquaintance with these narratives, and the 'lost' bestselling novels are only discovered and enjoyed through film.

At its best an adaptation on screen can re-envision a well-worn narrative for a new audience inhabiting a very different cultural environment, and their relationship to the 'origin' may itself change enormously. An adaptation may be an act of criticism and reparation simultaneously; a text may well have outlived its usefulness or become too tired for contemporary tastes – an anecdotal example springs to mind. After we spoke to Andrew Davies about his TV adaptation of *Bleak House* and then watched the serial on television we both re-read the novel only to find that Davies's revisioning of Esther, his removal of her sometimes gratingly self-effacing narrative voice, made Dickens's Esther jar unbearably with the pleasures of other aspects of the novel as well as other narrative voices.[28] What Davies is addressing directly is Dickens's tendency to sentimentalise his central female characters to the obliteration of a convincing motivation for their behaviour. In Davies's *Bleak House* the burden of Esther's indebtedness to Jarndyce is made more manifest and this contemporary take on the relationship between ward and guardian foregrounds the unsavoury implications of a middle-aged man who attempts to transform his relationship with a young woman from father-figure to lover (in his recent *Little Dorrit* for BBC TV, 2008, he also takes on Edzard's 1988 film, reducing the age discrepancy between Arthur Clennan and Little Dorrit, possibly to discourage rather than encourage a reading of the relationship as akin to father and daughter).

For Naremore, theorists that look on 'adaptation as translation' (Bluestone, McFarlane) tend to always return to the fidelity debate and, 'here as elsewhere, the study of adaptation stops at the water's edge, as if it were hesitant to move beyond literary formalism and ask more interesting questions'.[29] In 2000 Naremore noted a certain *impasse* in adaptation studies and suggested the need to move beyond the parameters of the classic literary text to popular culture, also asserting that we need to look at 'recycling, remaking and every other form of retelling' which for him would result in the end of adaptation studies as we know it, and 'become part of a general theory of repetition, and adaptation study will move from the margins to the center of contemporary media studies'.[30] André Bazin, whose 'Adaptation, or the Cinema as Digest' also included in Naremore's collection, notes as others do, that the custom of adaptation is as old as culture and simply takes on new forms, as new media can do certain things better or differently than others (photos of paintings rather than engravings of them, for instance). This process is never simply in need of aesthetic justification or sense of purpose: it represents a nexus of economic, ideological and artistic responses and film adaptation, by its sheer expense, requires the acceptance of its investors. Bazin himself imagines a time when the literary author will be decentralised and speculates that in a future period all narrative forms will receive more democratic critical responses: 'the (literary?) critic of the year 2050 would find not a novel out of which a play and a film had been "made", but rather a single work reflected through three art forms, an artistic pyramid with three sides, all equal in the eyes of the critic'[31] – is this a utopian or dystopian thought? Given it was written in 1948, it seems realistic in its prediction of the length of time if might take for such a paradigm shift across the disciplines of film and literary studies.

For writers such as Robert B. Ray it is as if the golden age of adaptations studies is already over just as the public hunger for adaptations soar, if we take seriously his claim that the field of adaptation studies 'fell into disrepute'[32] during the 1980s and 1990s. And consider the picture he paints of a hybrid subject bedevilled by its location at the intersection of film and literary studies and, in the United States, responsive to the vagaries of the tenure system which, he claims, caused a move away from the lengthy theoretical project towards the 20-page article, and hence the proliferation of case studies which Ray suggests do not take us further than industry knowledge itself, where 'long before its critics... Hollywood recognized the perpetual interchange between film and writing and its role in creating (or controlling) meaning'.[33] Robert Stam's contribution is to further unravel the prejudices against film which is still almost always portrayed as a 'lesser' art form, unable to provide point-of-view or complex character psychology, for example, but he conceptualises the film as 'multitrack' to suggest its dimensions far outscope that of the literary text:

> The novel has a single material of expression, the written word, whereas the film has at least five tracks: moving photographic image, phonetic sound, music, noises, and written materials. In this sense, the cinema has not lesser, but rather greater resources for expression than the novel, and this is independent of what actual filmmakers have done with these resources.[34]

Stam's quasi-formalist summary of cinema's potential can be added to its cultural and ideological reach, and here we might want to refer back to Cohen's view of the relationship of film to literature as the 'dynamics of exchange' (as in his book's subtitle), giving cinema the dominant role in stirring literature out of its ageing complacency: 'it was as though the cinema had become a huge magnet whose field exerted on other arts like the novel an attraction as powerful and as ineluctable as gravity'.[35]

So-called 'classic' literary adaptations are usually those which take mainly pre-twentieth-century writings as their prompt and create something which re-enacts the historical space of the hypotext so that what we are first reminded of is the historical location of the text, rather than its major themes and motivations. In this way the term 'classic adaptation' speaks of a genre identity of its own and perhaps a number of sub-genres such as the 1980s and 1990s TV classic serial; the return-to-origins film version (such as *Mary Shelley's Frankenstein*, 1994). They have been the source of fairly sustained academic study because they allow further consideration of well-loved texts which are also staples of a liberal education, and whether or not we actually believe any more that reading great works of literature makes us a better person, we turn to such adaptations sometimes for vicarious edification. 'Good' adaptations have in the past been seen as aids to literary textual understanding and a significant part of early adaptations study concerned itself almost solely with adaptations which related to 'worthy' literary sources. Some 'classic' texts are naturally more 'classic' than others, and different conceptions of authorial identities lend their imprint to the scope of subsequent adaptations. In this way the 'lawks-a-daisy' light comedy of the 1940 Robert Z. Leonard *Pride and Prejudice* initiates a 'house style' for Austen talkie adaptations, where romance and comedy and the central couple are foregrounded above social context, class and gender concerns; the Brontës

are clustered together and the moody chiaroscuro cinematography of
William Wyler's *Wuthering Heights* (1939), starring Laurence Olivier,
and Robert Stevenson's *Jane Eyre* (1944), starring Orson Welles,
owes more to the gothic tendency in film; Dickens's techniques in
characterisation are seem to require grotesques and the films are
populated by character actors, and cityscapes form a powerful interpretative part of the narrative. Such house styles extend, of course, to
music choices, costume, and the reliance on a certain 'camp' of stars
in any given generation; and literary 'classics', instead of being freed
from their authors in the melting pot of cross-media transformation,
become visually fixed to an imagined identity just a strong as the name
on the title page of the printed book.

   Of course numerous adaptation critics have lauded the 'Death of
Author' – sometimes in quite literal terms – and many want from that
assertion a release from the tyranny of intentionalism, yet Hutcheon,
while seeing the need to turn away from the author as arbiter of meaning, still suggests that in adaptation, intentions 'are recoverable, and
their traces are visible in the text. ... adaptation teaches us that if we
cannot talk about the creative process, we cannot fully understand
the urge to adapt and therefore perhaps the very process of adaptation. We need to know "why".'[36] Hutcheon's 2006 book is structured
around questions such as the how, the what, where, or when, and in
terms of the audience experience of adaptation she emphasises the
pleasure of both repetition and difference:'Like ritual, this kind of repetition brings comfort, a fuller understanding, and the confidence that
comes with the sense of knowing what is about to happen next';[37] she
acknowledges, too, how important fan communities are to the adaptation industry (if one can say there is such a thing). Moreover, and
perhaps linked to more nuanced debates around fidelity, Hutcheon
notes the important educational value placed upon some adaptations
and their or the book's paratexts: 'Today, hardly a book or a movie
aimed at school-aged children does not have its own Web site, complete with advice and materials for teachers';[38] also, making of movies,
novelisations and video games can all contribute to the 'backstory'
of the adaptation. If we haven't read the adapted text but know of
it by reputation, especially with classic texts, 'we tend to experience
the adaptation through the lenses of the adapted work, as a kind of
palimpsest'.[39]In her conclusion Hutcheon notes the important afterlife an adaptation can give another text in a cycle that reminds us, in
Stam's words, that 'literature pays indirect, and begrudging, homage

to film's popularity, while film pays homage to literature's prestige'.[40] The following chapters look at both sides of the debate: from the perspective of film enthusiasts and from the vantage of those with literary affiliations, but with a clear eye on the afterlife of adaptation – the spaces in which the 'dynamics of exchange' occur.

2

Film on Literature: Film as the New Shakespeare

This chapter looks at literary adaptations from the perspective of film, especially in the early period of cinema, setting forth some of the reasons why the form was so disdained by so many film-makers and film enthusiasts. The formulation 'Literature on Screen' or 'Shakespeare on Screen' implies a superiority of one art over another, and this view that literature/Shakespeare is the pre-eminent party is, by no means, universally shared and is especially evident outside English and Drama studies. Our argument departs from 'traditional' Shakespeare on Screen studies in its attempt to locate Shakespeare on film within a larger field of adaptation studies, considering that Shakespeare on film seems to have established itself as an area in its own right, with little or no heed of the wider context of studies in adaptations.[1] In the light of the artistic claims made for cinema in the first half of the twentieth century, together with the negative reception to film adaptations of literature, especially adaptations of dramatic literature, this chapter examines how feature-length films of *Hamlet*, in this period, compare and contrast theatrical and filmic styles. In some instances, it seems, the usual trajectory of Shakespeare on film is subtly reversed: that is, Shakespeare on film becomes, if only momentarily, film on Shakespeare.[2]

Early in its history, cinema, possibly due to its creation by production teams (rather than a single artist) and to its reliance on technology, was regarded by many as an industry, not an art form, and therefore considered a low form of entertainment, not to be compared in any way with arts such as painting or literature. In *Theatre and Film*

(1936), theatre historian Allardyce Nicoll joins in the challenge to this still-prevalent assumption and draws parallels between the opposition to Elizabethan drama and the academic snubbing of film as mass-produced, commercially motivated entertainment. Indeed, for Nicoll, film is the new Shakespeare. Arguing for a higher valuation of cinema, Nicoll compares the Elizabethan and Jacobean refusal to publish plays (for commercial reasons) with the lack of availability and valuation of screenplays, which he predicts will be soon remedied, whereupon, in his words, 'Poetry must enter the cinema.'[3] Coming from a literary and theatrical background, Nicoll instinctively wants to elevate the writer of films from a position of obscurity and proposes that the screenplay writers (whose position he likens to the condition of Shakespeare and his contemporaries) need to be better credited and valued if cinema is to be regarded as art.

This comparison of the film industry from its beginning to the 1930s to the original conditions of Shakespeare's productions is apt and a number of further parallels can be drawn. William Hunter, writing in 1932, addresses the problem of popular film appealing to the lowest denominator, by referring to Shakespeare who, rather than 'withdrawing aesthetic sophistication', appealed at 'a number of different levels of response, so that the most vulgar and the most refined were both satisfied'.[4] The analogy of film appealing to the masses and to the multi-layered meanings inherent in Elizabethan drama is also made by social observer, Margaret Farrand Thorp, writing in 1939. Seeing the Shakespearean approach to the masses as the solution for the movies, Thorp writes that 'the movies seem to be quite capable of proceeding on two levels as Elizabethan tragedy: poetry and psychology for the gentlemen's gallery, action and blood for the pit'.[5] Thorp touches on the very forte of adaptations that, by their nature, strive to appeal to audiences both familiar and unfamiliar with their literary sources. Film critic, theorist and co-founder of *Cahiers du cinéma*, André Bazin, equates the absence of an authorial presence in cinema with earlier literary conditions, like those of Shakespeare, in which the 'author' was of little, or no consequence; Bazin reminds us in 1948 what Roland Barthes observes 20 years later in his famous essay, 'The Death of the Author'. For Bazin:

> the ferocious defence of literary works is, to a certain extent, aesthetically justified; but we must also be aware that it rests on a rather recent, individualistic conception of the 'author' and of the 'work', a conception that was far from being ethically rigorous in the seventeenth century and that started to become legally defined only at the end of the eighteenth.[6]

The insignificance of the author is just one of many parallels drawn between the Shakespearean and film production in John Madden's *Shakespeare in Love* (1998). While the film makes much of the rehearsal, Tiffany Stern explains how actors in Shakespeare's period didn't actually rehearse as a group, but were individually coached, coming together for the first time in the first performance of the play, with the 'book-holder', like a conductor in an orchestra, directing them offstage.[7] As in a movie, the final production was not masterminded by a single individual (least of all, the author); Shakespeare's perform- ances were the products of many, not of a single writer, and, akin to actors in a film, Shakespeare's players, prior to the first production, would be unaware of the full picture, that is, what happens in the play as a whole.

In his extraordinary book, Nicoll predicts that, like Shakespeare, film will eventually be given the artistic reputation it deserves so long as it doesn't merely 'ransack' and 'cull' (his words) the great works of literature.[8] In other words, in order to succeed and be the 'new Shakespeare', Nicoll contends that film must be independent of lit- erature. Essentially, the attitude to the combination of literature and film in the early part of the twentieth century can be divided into three positions: those film 'purists' who wanted nothing to do with literature; those who found in literature analogies and methodologies applicable to film and those who adapted not just literary techniques and stylistic devices, but an entire literary text.

Film on Shakespeare

Nicoll recounts the early opposition to filming literature and drama by those who felt cinema should stand on its own, unaided by literature.[9] Filmmaker Sergei Eisenstein found in 'cinematic literature', which includes Shakespeare, Zola, Dickens, Balzac and Flaubert, among others, emphatically not sources but 'schools' (to use his term) for film-makers.[10] Eisenstein was not in favour of direct borrowing from literature, but rather, as he puts it, 'as a matter of studying all elements that constitute their specificity'.[11] In one of his most famous essays, he compares the filmic techniques of American director David Wark Griffith with the literary devices of Charles Dickens:

> From that steely, observing glance, which I remember from my meeting with him [Griffith], to the capture *en passant* of key details or tokens – indications of character, Griffith has all this in as much a Dickens-esque

sharpness and clarity as Dickens, on his part, had cinematic 'optical quality,' 'frame composition,' 'close-up,' and the alteration of emphasis by special lenses.[12]

Eisenstein sees Dickens's writing as filmic, in its interest in urbanisation, its visual images, montages and close-ups.[13] In a slightly defensive tone, Eisenstein suggests that 'Dickens and the whole ancestral array going back as far as the Greeks and Shakespeare' are 'reminders that both Griffith and our cinema prove our origins to be not solely in Edison and his fellow inventors, but as based on an enormous cultural past'.[14] For Eisenstein and his followers, film is the new literature (as it is, more precisely for Nicoll, 'the new Shakespeare'). Griffith is praised for narrating visually, translating stylistic devices and techniques from Dickens, importantly not for 'borrowing' his stories wholesale. Nonetheless, since the inception of cinema, film-makers chose to adapt or 'borrow' stories from novels and plays, partially because some of it, such as the novels of Flaubert, Dickens and Zola, was regarded, as Eisenstein points out, as 'cinematic literature'. The stories were well known and thus the narratives were easy to follow, but also, by linking these authors' names to film, the cultural value of cinema was uplifted.

The first film of a Shakespeare play, *King John,* was defended by W.T. Smedley, the managing director of British Biograph, in an interview in *The Westminster Gazette* in 1899 as evidence of the potential intellectual value of cinema:

> Continuing, the chairman asserted that such classical reproductions of Shakespeare would remove the stigma, which, justly or unjustly, at present is apt to be cast on moving pictures. The public taste in this direction is, I was assured, rapidly mounting to a higher and better level; with the introduction of Shakespeare and other perfectly harmless subjects on the films of the machines the craving for 'something a little risky' would be eradicated.[15]

More prominently Frank L. Dyer encouraged the classic adaptation as a way of uplifting the cultural status of the cinema: 'When the works of Dickens and Victor Hugo, the poems of Browning, the plays of Shakespeare and stories from the Bible are used as a basis for moving pictures, no fair-minded man can deny that the art is being developed along the right lines.'[16] Dyer reveals the inferiority complex present in early cinema and the need, in some quarters, for it to draw from literature in order to enhance its reputation, both intellectually and morally. Dyer was attempting to placate a growing paranoia in which cinema was regarded as a corrupt and immoral influence on the general public, a paranoia still present in the 1920s, with film-makers like D.W. Griffith having to defend their art with essays such as 'Are Motion Pictures Destructive of Good Taste?' (1923). Film adaptations of literature were clearly utilised to assuage a general concern about the morality of movies, a concern that eventually resulted in the United States in the Hays Production Code that, from the early 1930s to the early 1950s, imposed tight regulation on the content of commercial cinema to protect what was deemed a vulnerable and all-too impressionable cinema audience. The argument 'for adaptation' was, clearly, unpopular with literary and film scholars as it assumed the purpose of both arts was purely moral. In *The Devil's Camera*, first published in 1932, R.G. Burnett and E.D. Martell see literature as rescuing film from 'filth and brutality':[17]

> No country has finer literature than England from which to take its themes. What films could be made from English history, from Chaucer and Shakespeare and Scott and Dickens and Wells and Chesterton! *Pilgrim's Progress* could be interpreted on the screen as nowhere else. What Englishman would not want to see it? Consider *Gulliver's Travels*, and *The Napoleon of Notting Hill*. American sex and gangster themes would dwindle into nothingness beside them.[18]

The argument that film needs literature in order to achieve moral worthiness could hardly be popular with film-makers, and undoubtedly contributed to the cold shoulder presented to literature on screen in the first half of the twentieth century. Here as well we sense nationalist tensions emerging where claims are made for the morally uplifting potential of specifically *English* literature. As Graham Greene observed later in the century, film adaptation has a moral, not an aesthetic purpose. Reviewing *Romeo and Juliet* in 1936, he admits that he is 'less than ever convinced that there is an aesthetic justification for filming Shakespeare at all'. While observing that it is impossible to listen to the poetry while looking at the film, he writes 'that there might be a social justification I do not dispute; by all means let Shakespeare, even robbed of half his drama and three quarters of his poetry be mass produced'.[19] For Greene, adaptations of Shakespeare have a social purpose, to teach 'the great middle class a little about Shakespeare's plays'.[20]

While film has undoubtedly achieved its early ambition of attaining artistic recognition equivalent to the more traditional art forms, literature on screen has some way to go in this direction. Prejudice can still be felt in the field of film adaptations, a prejudice that the purist school of film-makers perpetuated, in their insistence that films that 'steal' narrative structures from literature render the adaptation dependent upon and inferior to their literary counterpart. Luigi Pirandello, for one, argued vehemently that 'the cinema must free itself of literature, leaving narrative to novels and the theatre'.[21] The coming of sound augmented the hostility to adaptations voiced by the film purists, such as those writing for the magazine *Close Up* (1927–33), whose aim was to defend cinema as an art, separate but equal to literature, art and music. Writing in *Close Up* in 1929, Jean Lenauer, an eventual convert to sound, originally feared that sound would 'degrade' and 'deform' film by turning it into theatre.[22] As William Hunter summarised in 1932, before the coming of sound, film had begun 'to diverge from its theatrical origins, towards something individual and independent'.[23] For opponents of the narrative film, sound was bad news, throwing film back to its theatrical roots. The 'dialogue films' were scorned by documentary film-maker Paul Rotha in 1930 as they were seen as 'simply reduction to absurdity of the attempt to join two separate arts which, by their essential nature, defy synchronization'.[24] The position that film should be seen and not heard accounts for the longstanding prejudicial reception of adaptations of literature, especially drama.

By 1950, film had made it into Arnold Hauser's last volume of *The Social History of Art* that concludes with 'the Film Age'. Hauser, however, excludes the narrative film or adaptation from the accolade of art. He complains about the loss of ' "cinematic" means of expression' to narrative: 'film, whose public is on the average level of the petty bourgeois, borrows these formulae from the light fiction of the upper middle class and entertains the cinema-goers of today with the dramatic effects of yesterday'.[25] For Hauser, sound hurled film back to a reliance on narrative, which, he complains, became increasingly infantilising and predictable: 'films in which people simply walk out of one social stratum into another'.[26] To summarise, literature on screen has a history of being rejected by both the 'defenders' of literature who felt it contributed to a decline in reading and thinking but, more subtly and persuasively, these movies were spurned by film-makers and film enthusiasts, indeed writers themselves, who wanted film to have an identity all of its own. Literature, especially drama on film, it seems, belonged to neither literature and theatre, nor to film studies. Herbert Read, in 'The Poet and the Film', takes issues with Salvador Dali's 'down with the literary film' stance, arguing that 'those people who deny that there can be any connection between the scenario and literature seem to me to have a wrong conception, not so much of the film as of literature' (published 1945).[27] This prejudice towards any alliance between film and literature, that Read so astutely identifies, can still be felt today.

Adaptations were frequently seen to be trying to be something they weren't, regarded as commercially successful but artistically misguided attempts to achieve cultural and, perhaps more infuriatingly to filmmakers and film enthusiasts, moral value. They were seen to sacrifice both film and literature for the sake of a cheap reproduction. Nonetheless, some classic adaptation afforded film-makers an opportunity to reflect upon the very process of the cinematic appropriation of literature, enabling an on-screen dialogue with these literary sources. If we take Nicoll's suggestion that film is the new Shakespeare a stage further, then we have to concede the obvious point that Shakespeare himself was an adaptor of others' works and, as Shakespeare has more than demonstrated, an adaptation is rarely a straightforward copy. André Bazin, a champion of adaptations in the 1950s, preached that in post-1940 adaptation, literature was not experienced *as* cinema, but *through* it. Rather than divide or diminish the literary text, Bazin courageously claimed that good adaptations give the lie to the view that they can be nothing but slothful copies. A voice in the wilderness, he argued that, rather than being reduced beyond recognition, a novel or play could be multiplied by cinema.[28] Film adaptation or what was often regarded as 'impure cinema' can, as Brian McFarlane has remarked over fifty years after Bazin, engage with literature in ways that involve questions of authorship, the present's relationship to the past and the contemporary relevance of the adapted text.[29] Literature – including Shakespeare – on screen is normally interpreted in terms of its understanding of or reverence to its source, but as Julie Sanders has stressed, this is only half of the picture: adaptations provide 'as many opportunities for divergence as adherence, for assault as well as homage'.[30]

The very first films included adaptations of classic literature, such as *King John* (1899), *Uncle Tom's Cabin* (1903), *Hamlet* (1907), and even the Bible. The portrayal of 'the word of God' without the word was an amazing feat in the early twentieth century; picturing Christ, especially, on screen, was potentially iconoclastic in the extreme. As Judith Buchanan has described, silent film-makers astonishingly overcame the religious opposition in visually depicting Christ in the production of a number of biblical films in the silent era. Buchanan notes that in Cecil B. DeMille's popular film, *The King of Kings* (1927), the appearance of Christ is strategically delayed and we see him through the eyes of a girl who has just been miraculously cured of blindness – the emergence of the face is 'like a stylized rehearsal of the coming of cinema itself'. [31] This sequence sums up the long held but often unvoiced attitude of film-makers to their literary sources; far from being deferential, and unworthy, when it comes to adaptations, film often presents itself in meta-adaptive (for some, blasphemous) moments, as having the potential to transform and even replace the 'original', not simply to 'copy'.

Screening theatre in *Hamlet*

On the face of it, to adapt Shakespeare to the silent screen seems almost as profane an act, but one that nevertheless was attempted from the earliest period of film history. Of all of Shakespeare's plays, *Hamlet* is, probably, the most frequently adapted. At the time of writing, there are 104 versions listed on the Internet Movie Database, and how film, from the early twentieth century to the beginning of the twenty-first century, approaches what is one of the most respected of literary works, tells us much about trends in the film industry's appropriation and relationship with the so-called literary classics. In 'The Mousetrap', the play within the play, Shakespeare himself grapples with the subject of adaptation, and when translated to film, the scene is often transformed into a self-reflexive account of the relation between film and theatre, representationalism and realism, adaptation and source text. What Shakespeare is confronting in the play are two types of representation, an earlier more stylised theatricality, reflected in the formal language with constraining rhyming couplets which often distort the order of the words,[32] contrasted to the more free and varied approach of his own period. The play within a play is itself an adaptation by Hamlet who inserts 'a speech of some dozen lines, or sixteen lines' (2.2.476–7) into a play 'written in very choice Italian' (3.2.255). An obvious point, but one worth stressing, is that on screen the play within the play becomes a play within a film, and unavoidably asks the rhetorical question to its viewers as to which form is preferred (film or theatre?). Given a climate of artistic hostility to adaptations, in particular, theatrical cinema, the seemingly unavoidable meeting of theatre and film in these adaptations provide opportunities to foreground the theatre/film debate.

The history of *Hamlet* on screen commences in 1900 with Sarah Bernhardt notoriously fleetingly performing the title role on screen.

Pioneering film-maker Georges Méliès produced a *Hamlet* in 1907 (starring himself as Hamlet), the same year as his *Le Rêve de Shakespeare* or *La Mort de Jules César*, in which the 'Great Méliès', magician turned filmmaker, plays the part of Shakespeare himself. It's hard not to speculate that Méliès's decision to play the part of the playwright is an implicit assertion that the filmmaker is 'the new Shakespeare', but, as the film is no longer available, it's impossible to know how far this can be taken. Unfortunately, both Méliès's Shakespeare films are lost, and this is the case with most of the films of *Hamlet* produced in the early period of cinema of which there are an estimated 41;[33] from the surviving descriptions, most of these delete or diminish the play within a play and extend, through visualisation, the suicide of Ophelia (which is only reported in the play); in short, from an albeit mostly second-hand overview, these films tend to erase the play's theatrical origins in an effort to make Shakespeare more cinematic. There are only three surviving feature-length films in this period: a British film of 1913 directed by E. Hay Plumb and starring Johnston Forbes-Robertson; an Italian version, *Amleto* (1917), directed by Eleuterio Rodolfi with Ruggero Ruggeri as Hamlet; and a German film, *Hamlet: The Drama of Revenge* (1921), with the acclaimed Danish actress, Asta Nielsen, as Hamlet.

The least cinematic of all is the 1913 Gaumont-Hepworth *Hamlet*, starring Johnston Forbes-Robertson, filmed, essentially, to preserve the 60-year-old actor's performance. As Emma Smith has shown, the production is uneasy about itself as film and, in its publicity materials, took every opportunity to stress that the production was based on its illustrious stage production. Filmed before 'theatrical' was a term of disparagement for cinema, Forbes-Robertson's angular figure and sunken, deeply expressive eyes make for a very charismatic and quintessentially theatrical Hamlet.[34] The sequences are very long and the static camera is often aimed at an arch that frames the actors, as if they were on a stage. Unnervingly, the actors' mouths are continually moving as if they're actually speaking the words. Speech is visually present and therefore noticeably absent; the silent but prominently moving mouths of the actors are a visible reminder to the viewer that Shakespeare's words are missing. While shot both inside and outside, including sequences in woodlands and on a coastline, the film, nonetheless, announces itself as piece of theatre, especially in the play-within-the-play sequence. The play is staged in the distance, framed by an arch, with Hamlet stretched on the floor in the foreground, gesturing towards the players. Their brief, framed and silent performance is like a moving painting, recalling a film as much as a stage performance. Hamlet competes with the players for centre stage, with the audience, like spectators watching a tennis match, exchanging their gaze back and forth across a diagonal axis, from Hamlet to the play and finally to Hamlet, with the theatrical Hamlet visually triumphing over the lacklustre 'filmic' performance of the players. Almost perversely, as Emma Smith has argued, the film repudiates itself in its celebration of the theatrical.

The next feature-length film, *Amleto* (1917), has been described as a 'halfway style between film and theatre, eschewing a more conventional style'.[35] The sequences are shorter, there is more variety of shots and the viewer is not tantalised by the sight of mouths constantly moving, thereby drawing attention to the missing words. The emphasis on the visual is noticeable in the death of Ophelia, witnessed by Gertrude, and clearly influenced by the famous Millais portrait of *Ophelia* (1852). The film ends, like the Forbes-Robertson film, with the crowning of the dead Hamlet, but this is the only resemblance to the earlier film. Hamlet, played by Italian actor Ruggero Ruggeri, advises the overly dramatic actors to tone down their gestures; in short, to behave more like film actors. This is advice that they clearly don't take, given their exaggeratedly stylised and unemotional performance. The emphasis, in this sequence, is on the audience and, implicitly, the clear superiority of the film to the theatre.

While the Forbes-Robertson *Hamlet* aimed to divorce itself from cinema, seemingly in order to enhance its value, Svend Gade and Heinz Schall's 1921 *Hamlet: The Drama of Vengeance*, starring 40-year-old Danish actress Asta Nielsen, undoubtedly puts cinema before both theatre and Shakespeare. Described by Kenneth Rothwell in *A History of Shakespeare on Screen* as striking 'a great blow in liberating the Shakespeare movie from theatrical and textual dependency and moving toward the filmic',[36] the film, inspired by Edward P. Vining's eccentric interpretation of the play in *The Mystery of Hamlet* (1881), in which it is proposed that Hamlet was actually female, seems to defy the playtext at every turn. It opens with the birth of Hamlet and the wounding of Hamlet Senior in battle. Eager to secure the succession and fearful of the fate of her husband, Gertrude decides to disguise her child as a male and informs her husband, on his return, that she has done so. Gade makes clear that Gertrude is having an affair with a dishevelled and exceedingly seedy Claudius long before Hamlet Senior's death. Much of the film takes place in Wittenberg, where Hamlet is joined by a debauched Laertes and a forgiving Fortinbras (after some reservation, they become friends), and we see him/her meeting and falling hopelessly in love with Horatio. In Denmark, much to Hamlet's chagrin, Horatio falls in love with (a very large) Ophelia. This *Hamlet* becomes a story of the unrequited love between Horatio, dressed, for the most part, in extravagant chiffon doublets with billowing sleeves and matching hats, and Hamlet, who is attired throughout in more masculine and subdued costumes, always black. Hamlet ends up in Normandy, where he/she unashamedly delivers Rosencrantz and Guildenstern to his/her friend, Fortinbras for execution; Fortinbras then accompanies Hamlet, with a large army, back to Denmark. In another of the many departures from the play, Hamlet manages to set fire to Claudius and his drinking mates, leaving it to a not very maternal Gertrude to envenom the sword and plant the poison for Hamlet to drink. Tragically, Horatio discovers only after Hamlet dies that she is a woman, when his hand falls accidentally on her breast.

While the film leaves you asking a number of questions (such as: why wasn't Claudius informed that Hamlet was a woman; what happens to Laertes after he kills Hamlet; why doesn't Hamlet tell Horatio that she's a woman?), there are some stunning sequences and the film has a gothic and balletic quality throughout that powerfully conveys Hamlet's sense of isolation and loneliness. Of the three feature-length films of the silent era, as Robert Hamilton Ball observes, 'the least Shakespearean *Hamlet* becomes the best *Hamlet* film'.[37] Prior to the performance of the play within the play, Nielsen's Hamlet attempts to tone down the ridiculously exaggerated gestures of the players by physically restraining their arm-swinging. Asta Nielsen, renowned for her restraint as an actress, visually mocks the 'sawing of the air' in a scene that pointedly distinguishes the theatrical from the filmic. The performance of the play itself is predictably comical in its extreme and formulaic gesturing, underlining its artificiality, which is in direct contrast to the more visually stimulating reaction to the play by Claudius and, especially, by Hamlet, whose dark angular figure is shown crawling across the frame, referencing the famous crawl of nineteenth-century Shakespearean actor Edmund Kean,[38] visually stealing the show.

The scene is utterly transformed in Laurence Olivier's 1948 film. In *Henry V,* Olivier privileges film over theatre through juxtaposition; the film begins with a performance at the Globe, moves out to a painted set, and then to location shooting, reflecting Jack Jorgens's three types of adaptation, the theatrical, realist and filmic.[39] In *Hamlet,* Olivier blends theatre with film so that the two styles are virtually indistinguishable. His players manage to 'hold the mirror up to nature', as is evident when Olivier's Hamlet places the blond wig on the boy actor who becomes, for a moment, transformed into a replica of Ophelia, as is evident from Olivier's disturbed reaction. The dumbshow is featured on a stage that is part of the churchlike interior of the film space, the actors are dressed in similar costumes to the characters watching them, and the players' reactions are not forced, but natural. The boundaries between the stage and audience space are hardly perceptible. The sequence stresses the perfect blending of theatre and film, Shakespeare and cinema.

In Soviet director Grigori Kozintzev's *Gamlet* (1964), the play is performed outside with the sea in the background; the lack of architectural determination gives the play a filmic rather than theatrical quality. With heavily made-up actors and stylised gestures, the play within a play is more like a film from the silent era (reminiscent of scenes from *Amleto*) than one contemporary to the production. This is a film in a film rather than a play within a film, reflecting on the improvements in Shakespeare on screen from the silent period to mid-century, rather than on film's triumph over theatre. In this film, the theatrical style has seemingly vanished.

Zeffirelli's bewilderingly cut *Hamlet* of 1990 includes much of the 'Get thee to a nunnery' scene in the sequence that opens with 'The play's the thing' speech. Here, like in Kozintzev's *Gamlet,* the actors are clearly distinguished from the Danish court by their heavy make-up, ill-fitting costumes, wooden gestures and overly stressed verse speaking. The play gradually recedes into the background as the sequence progresses, the focus being on the doomed love of Hamlet and Ophelia and Claudius's mounting distress. The abrupt closure of the play is instantly followed by a face-to-face confrontation between Claudius and the vampire-like player of Lucianus, clutching the vial of poison; for Claudius the play indeed 'holds the mirror up to nature', as Zeffirelli, through the use of close-up, transforms the theatrical into the filmic.

Kenneth Branagh's 'full text' 1996 film turns Hamlet into a theatrical performer, screaming out his lines for the entire assembly to hear. In contrast, the Player King and Player Queen are soft-spoken and intimate; unlike in the previous films, we see them in close-up, the camera virtually erasing the audience altogether. Indeed the pensive and emotive Player King, played by veteran actor Charlton Heston, is metamorphosed into something like Plato's Philosopher King; 'The Murder of Gonzago' is not mocked, but applauded for the beauty of its poetry, culminating in a cutaway shot to the actual murder. Unlike

the Zeffirelli version, where filmic space replaces the dull artificiality
of the theatre, here the theatrical performance is valorised: it inspires
and leads us into the filmic.

Finally, Michael Almereyda's 'Generation-X' *Hamlet,* starring Ethan
Hawke, daringly omits theatre altogether; *The Mousetrap* is a compi-
lation video/film, featuring 1950s sitcoms, a silent film, *Cleopatra,* and
segments from the pornographic film, *Deep Throat* (1977), framed by
a red rose seen opening at the beginning and decomposing at the end.
The rose not only alerts the viewer to the ephemeral nature of beauty,
it also serves to remind us of what film can do that theatre can't in the
portrayal of the acceleration of motion. The sequence portraying a
crowning of a king strikes the final blow for Claudius and brings the
'entertainment' to an end. The video cover is shown on camera prior
to the screening, revealing '"The Mousetrap", a tragedy by Hamlet
Prince of Denmark'. Rather than the title of the film, as is usually the
case, Hamlet's name is larger than the rest of the script, visually confusing author and title, suggesting that the play within the play is *Hamlet*
itself. Rather than assaulting the theatrical origins of the film (as in
Gade or Zeffirelli), or paying homage (as in Olivier and Branagh), this
film ignores them altogether. The film's blatant erasure of theatricality is interpreted by Robert Shaughnessy as typical of Shakespeare
on screen in the early twenty-first century.[40] The film is undoubtedly
more interested in itself as an adaptation of other films of *Hamlet* than
as a version of Shakespeare's play. At the beginning of the twenty-first
century, the debate between theatre and film, articulated in all the previous films discussed here, has now vanished entirely.

We have considered the intellectual snobbery, from the perspective
of film, that has accompanied literature on screen, especially dramatic
literature on screen, owing to a long-held assumption that translations
of literature to screen are invariably either deliberate or unwitting dec-
larations of cinema's inferiority. Surveying theatre on screen in adaptations of *Hamlet* from the beginning of the twentieth century reveals
another story; arguably, while some use film as an act of homage to
their theatrical 'superior', others use it to assault, question or erase
the 'original' altogether. Far from being parasitical, some adaptations
provide sites of contestation and interrogation, returning rather than
borrowing, augmenting rather than culling from the 'original'. This is
film on theatre, not theatre on film, as film, for some of these adaptations of *Hamlet,* is, indeed, the new Shakespeare.

3

Literature on Film: Writers on Adaptations in the Early Twentieth Century

While the previous chapter reflected on attitudes to adaptations from the perspective of those in the early film business, this chapter looks at perceptions of adaptations from those connected to literary studies in the first part of the twentieth century. We address the seemingly inseparable intellectual and social opposition by writers to adaptations from the early twentieth century onwards, a snobbery that succeeded in withholding serious or sustained recognition of the field, as anything but an adjunct to the 'main business' of literary or film studies. The last section reflects on how recent work has interrogated long-held assumptions about film adaptations of literature, assumptions which, we argue, have their origins in social elitism as much as in a sense of intellectual unworthiness and which reflect deeply outdated views about the way we consume both film and literature in the twenty-first century.

While, as the last chapter revealed, defenders of film, such as Vachel Lindsay, who in 1915 rejected film adaptation of literary texts because these films were seen to proclaim cinema's dependency on literature, literary scholars found even more to dislike about cinematic adaptations of canonical texts. Historically, the dominant literary perspective on film, especially literary adaptations, has been one of hostility and is best summarised in what is probably the most famous attack on literature on screen: that of Virginia Woolf in her essay 'The Cinema' published in 1926. While the essay reveals Woolf's begrudging admiration for the cinema, particularly the subtleties of its visual codes, she has nothing but contempt for adaptations: 'So we lurch and lumber through the most famous novels of the world. So we spell them out in words of one syllable, written, too, in the scrawl of an illiterate schoolboy.'[1] Lurking behind the essay is a fear that adaptations are already threatening to destroy the civilised world as we know it; with a nod to Plato, she sees readers being replaced with 'savages of the twentieth century watching the pictures'.[2] Popularity is unproblematically associated in Woolf's essay with a necessary appeal to the lowest social/intellectual denominator, and 'popularity' here equates with cultural impoverishment.

Nonetheless, modernist writers, like Woolf herself, productively engaged with the cinema by absorbing cinematic devices in their writing. Charles Davy, writing in 1937, imagines screening a passage from Woolf's *The Years* in order to show how her work evokes the visual methods of cinema.[3] H.D., a regular contributor to *Close Up* (a magazine which was, of course, underpinned by a belief that film should be regarded as an art form) found in cinema new forms of poetic expression, as is evident in two poems entitled 'Projector' and 'Projector II'. In the latter poem, the experience of cinema is described in repetitious, short, blunt words, evocative of the mechanical clicking noise of a film projector.[4] H.D.'s poetic sect, the Imagists, have been identified as literary followers of the cinema.[5] The energy of film imagery is assimilated into their poetry in an attempt to achieve the aesthetic ambition that Joseph Conrad announced, in his preface to the *Nigger of the Narcissus* (1897), at the time of cinema's beginnings: 'My task which I am trying to achieve is, by the power of the written word, to make you hear, to make you feel – it is, before all, to make you *see*.'[6] Degrees of convergence between the two forms have been acknowledged as crucial to the development and speedy maturity of cinema. D.W. Griffith, regarded by Eisenstein as the shaper of American narrative film, looks back to the realist novels of the nineteenth century for technical inspiration and was said to come on to set every day with a Dickens novel in his hand.[7] For Eisenstein both Griffith's strengths and weaknesses were attributable to his love of that author. Yet what is latterly regarded by adaptation theorists as a fruitful and complex cross-fertilization of narrative forms was often perceived in terms of impurity, contamination or corruption.

As well as formal devices, cinema provided literature with new content: Pirandello's *Shoot* (1915), Horace McCoy's *They Shoot Horses, Don't They?* (1935), Nathanael West's *The Day of the Locust* (1939) and F. Scott Fitzgerald's *The Last Tycoon* (1941) are just some examples.[8] West's novel portrays Hollywood as a latter-day Babylon;

metaphorically embodied in the figure of 17-year-old Faye, the femme fatale whose doomed dream of making it big reflects the fatal attraction of Hollywood itself. Of all her suitors, the one who ultimately achieves Faye is the unworthy 'Mexican'; undeserving even of a name, the poor, uneducated immigrant is the villain of the piece. West portrays these 'savages of the human race' invading Hollywood, desecrating grand historical narratives, exchanging cultural and moral values with vulgarity and greed.

Tod Hackett, the putative central character of the novel, works in Hollywood as a set designer, although he still has a vocation as a painter. On one occasion he follows Faye through the film lot to watch her during filming of a piece entitled *Waterloo*. He notices at the onset of a filmed battle that the set depicting Mont St Jean is unfinished, its tenuous relationship to historical fact tinged by bathos:

> When the front rank of Milaud's heavy division started up the slope of Mont St Jean, the hill collapsed. The noise was terrific. Nails screamed with agony as they pulled out of joists. The sound of ripping canvas was like that of little children whimpering. Lath and scantling snapped as though they were brittle bones. The whole hill folded like an enormous umbrella and covered Napoleon's army with painted cloth.[9]

The film set is presented as utterly chaotic; and historical films as having little relationship to factual documentation. The sets are themselves hurriedly built with a view to being ripped down the next day to make way for the next feature. The 'actors' are presented as jobbing workers swift to depart the scene once their bit is over and with no palpable investment in film as art. While Tod offers an ironic and disdainful narrative viewpoint, West's victim of the Hollywood illusion, a model of decency and moral integrity, is Homer Simpson and, given current unavoidable associations with this now universally known name, West's satire inevitably backfires. The 'evil', unworthy inhabitants of Hollywood are not the 'traditional American', but an underclass, those previously on the edges of society, who West more often than not denies individuality, referring to them, not just by name, but also by type, such as 'the dwarf' or 'the Mexican'. Ultimately the riot, spurred by Homer's violence towards the boy Adore, exposes them in all their primal savagery, and we're reminded of an earlier description of one of Tod's paintings, *The Burning of Los Angeles*, which features such an apocalyptic scene. Robert Syvertan and Gloria Beatty in *They Shoot Horses, Don't They?*, both aspiring to join the film industry, join dozens of other couples in a marathon dance competition which they hope will gain them the notice of film actors or makers as they come to watch the spectacle. The centrepiece of the film is the inhuman marathon where competitors snatch 10 minutes of sleep in between bouts of dancing, and every evening the 'derby' pits couples against each other in exhausting circuits of the dance floor for bonuses, until they literally drop. Snatched moments of sexual congress under the grandstand are where dancers like Gloria attempt to ensure their elevation to stardom and McCoy includes, as characters, real-life movie stars such as Ruby Keeler who, in a reversal of their own role as spectacle, come to watch the agonising dancing of these hordes of hopefuls and offers an extra cash prize. As Charles Musser notes: 'Pain becomes spectacle. People come to see others who are more desperate than themselves, to see people struggle to stay standing, to ward off collapse. This spectacle is different from, indeed the reverse of, the spectacle offered by Warner Brothers' musicals.'[10] Musser also suggests that McCoy, in the conception of this novel, offers a reversal of the literature to film trajectory, moving from film to literature and using sources for this novel, *42nd Street* and *Gold Diggers of 1933* (both released in 1933), themselves either adaptations of novels or previous films and, in the case of the latter, making direct reference to the Depression. Unlike *Day of the Locust*, which ends with the climactic wave of violence of the 'mob', McCoy's violent ending is that prefigured at its opening – that of Robert finally agreeing to shoot Gloria (who has longed for death throughout the narrative) in an absurdist act which locates the tragedy in a more existential mode.

Fitzgerald's unfinished novel, *The Last Tycoon,* charts the increasing degradation of the author in Hollywood, where writing is done in teams at the behest of increasingly powerful producers. The novel opens with the narrator, the daughter of a Hollywood magnate, relating her English teachers' reactions to the cinema: 'some of the English teachers who pretended an indifference to Hollywood or its products really *hated* it. Hated it way down deep as a threat to their existence.'[11] The hatred for the cinematic text is rooted in both qualitative objections as well as in the factory-style method of production that inevitably results in the destruction of the Romantic conception of the author – destined to be replaced by the emergent 'auteurs', the film directors themselves, whereupon the 'pen' was passed to the director, resulting in the notion of 'La Camera-Stylo'. In spite of a cinematic programme of deauthorisation, established writers, such as F. Scott Fitzgerald, William Faulkner, Dylan Thomas and Aldous Huxley, actually worked as adapters; but for the most part (with the exception of some writers, like Graham Greene, who seems to have relished scriptwriting – even, almost blasphemously, declaring a film can be better than the book it's based on),[12] they admittedly did so out of avarice and with self-loathing;[13] Joseph Conrad, for instance, confessing to a friend that he is writing for cinema, explains: 'I am ashamed to tell you this ... but one must live'.[14]

Reworking Shakespeare's *The Tempest* in *Brave New World* (1932), Aldous Huxley savages film adaptation of Shakespeare through 'the feelies' (a thinly veiled version of the recently introduced 'talkies'); *Othello* becomes debased and unrecognisable as *Three Weeks in a Helicopter*, 'AN ALL-SUPER-SINGING, SYNTHETIC-TALKING, COLOURED, STEREOSCOPIC FEELY. WITH SYNCHRONIZED SCENT-ORGAN ACCOMPANIMENT'.[15] The repulsively seductive and debasing experience stimulated by this adaptation echoes Aldous Huxley's disgust, followed by self-loathing, upon experiencing *The Jazz Singer* ('I felt ashamed of myself for listening to such things, for even being a member of the species to which such things are addressed')[16]. In spite of his initial repugnance to 'the talkies', Huxley eventually warmed to the art of screenwriting, even settling down in Hollywood, adapting, with some pride, the likes of Jane Austen.[17] Even the film industry itself was often equally self-deprecating, openly admitting its own role in the desecration of a high culture and the intellectual impoverishment of the masses. Director Robert Rossen tells writer Robert Penn Warren that film adaptation is a process of simplification and dumbing down. Accounting for the script of *All the Kings Men* (1949), Rossen tells Warren: 'Son, when you are dealing with American movies you can forget, when you get to the end, anything like what you call Irony – then it's cops and robbers, cowboys and Indians.'[18]

Writers on film, such as Béla Balázs and Allardyce Nicoll, considered the script's potential to be regarded as a literary masterpiece, but the potential, if it existed at all, failed to be achieved. Balázs laments of film that 'the most important art of our time is that about which one need know nothing whatever',[19] and this statement still reflects the position of some 'literary' detractors of adaptation today, who feel perfectly equipped to make sweeping judgements on film with no real understanding of its formal qualities or potential at all. It's easy to understand the horror that greeted the earliest adaptations – words we still use today, like 'mutilate', 'betray', 'rob', 'ransack', 'cull' and 'desecrate', reveal that filming literature is often implicitly equated with perversity and criminality. In 1915, Walter Richard Eaton articulates the shock of the early reviewers of film adaptations when he sees one of his favourite theatre actresses on screen: '"Mrs. Friske in Tess" is announced in the motion-picture houses, but you almost weep when you witness that travesty on her poignant art, that reduction of a soul-gripping play to a poor pantomimic skeleton, like an illustrated report in a Hearst newspaper.'[20] According to Ella Shohat, the hostility to literature on screen has a theological origin, what she describes as 'an iconophobia rooted in the adoration of the word'.[21] Clearly, logocentricism accounts, to some degree, for the relatively short-lived literary hostility to film, but the still prevalent contempt for *literature* on film is also based on a sense of ownership. First, adaptations of 'great works of literature' were seen to devalue and potentially replace the literary original. As Woolf indicates, literature, reduced and simplified, appealed to 'the masses', and this fear of literature becoming popular resulting in social upheaval, or its potential contribution to the erosion of social boundaries, is behind much of the earlier criticism of adaptations. This is not to say that there were and have been some very poor adaptations of literature, adaptations that deserve to be forgotten, but these in no way pose any threat to the literary texts that they are based on. The real fear is that an adaptation will, as was the ambition of Walt Disney, usurp its literary source, becoming 'the original' in the minds of its audience.[22]

The loss of an authoritative 'original' is behind Jean-Paul Sartre's wry observation that the book exists as a relatively faithful commentary on the adaptation and the writer is the least important in the production hierarchy.[23] Adaptations are a product of what Sartre identifies as the institutionalisation of literature, where it is the audience rather than the author who dictates content. This view, held by many, is an extension of Plato's condemnation of the mass population by likening them to cave dwellers; never venturing outside, they see only reflections of the sun on a wall rather than gazing directly on the sun itself. And Plato's description of cave dwellers watching reflected lights in the dark in *The Republic*, bears an uncanny resemblance to spectators of film, especially viewers of adaptations, a gift for those opponents of literature on screen.

Replacing the author with a 'machine' was something that many, such as the adapter and novelist, Margaret Kennedy, in *The Mechanized Muse* (1942), found too difficult to accept: 'But there is really no such thing as screen *writing*. A script is not meant to be read, as novels, poems and plays are read. It is no more a work of theatre than it is the recipe for a pudding ... The trouble is that the recipe is never followed; the orchestra never plays the notes which the composer had set down.'[24] Kennedy sees the demise of the author as the root of the problem with literature on screen, imagining if Jane Austen were alive, she would have been asked to supply the 'story' of *Pride and Prejudice* without 'any of the idiomatic touches which lie in her dialogue'.[25] Like many, she believed that a group production could not be a work of art 'unless it has the stamp of one predominating, creative mind'. She observes: 'this single signature, in screen art, is at present the signature of the director'.[26]

While there were numerous literary champions of film as a new art form, few had anything good to say about adaptations in the early twentieth century. A number of literary figures made their views public. An essay in the *Bookman* in 1921, entitled 'The Motion Pictures: An Industry, Not an Art', regards movies as 'an institution by illiterates, of illiterates, and for illiterates',[27] and in this context illiteracy is another way of depicting and dismissing the working classes: 'Whether the movies in this country will ever attract the first-class artist is problematical. The field is held at present by ex-chauffeurs and ex-scene shifters who summarily reject all constructive criticism and are hostile to all ideas which they stigmatize as highbrow.'[28] Money, it appears, can only buy mediocrity, and George Bernard Shaw similarly pronounced that it is impossible to 'combine the pursuit of money with the pursuit of art'.[29] Agreeing, Shaw's biographer, Archibald Henderson, puts his finger on the problem – Americanisation and commercialisation are not the ingredients for quality cinema:

> But our happiest effects are achieved by having English duchesses impersonated by former cloak models, Italian counts by former restaurant waiters. In spite of this – the wonderful dinner parties of the European aristocracy, represented by people who have never gone out in good society even in a democracy, for example – the triumph of the American film is spectacular. The invasion of England and Europe is a smashing success. London, Paris, Berlin are placarded with announcements of American films: they are literally everywhere. *The Covered Wagon, Scaramouche, Hunchback of Notre Dame, Ten Commandments* ...[30]

Adaptations, and the people who make them, are here ridiculed for masquerading as a class above, foolishly rising above their status, and aspiring to do something they cannot possibly achieve. Arguing for the supremacy of the documentary film, John Grierson notes that film versions of 'Copperfields and Romeos' represent 'a special advance of the cinema into cultural grounds', but he compares these productions to prostitution, admitting 'we have always been snobs at heart'.[31] As one writer in the *English Review* opined in 1929, the public are being deceived into thinking that the reproduction is the 'real thing' – 'All the classics went through the machine, and in their reincarnations were represented as disseminators of "culture" among the populace.'[32] For Walter Benjamin, the dissemination of the adaptation has a democratising effect that should be celebrated rather than condemned. His 'Work of Art in the Age of Mechanical Reproduction' (1936) would come to gradually replace the objections to the popularisation and industrialisation of literature, articulated so frequently in the early twentieth century.

Significantly, the inaugural volume of F.R. Leavis's influential journal, *Scrutiny*, includes an article by William Hunter on film entitled 'The Art-Form of Democracy?', in which claims that directors such as Eisenstein could be regarded as second Shakespeares or Leonardos are summarily dismissed. Arguing that no film yet produced could merit the critical scrutiny of a good novel or poem, Hunter also questions the alleged democratic appeal of the cinema: 'The cinema is the art-form of "democracy" (the inverted commas are to admit that it might equally be called the art-form of capitalism).'[33] For Hunter, the films of his day, 'dreams of the shop girl and bank-clerk', are 'more thrillingly "real" when one can hear as well as see them'.[34] Last on the list for admission to the canon of English literature would be film adaptations of literary texts, appealing to the interests of 'bank-clerks' and 'shop girls' rather than the superior cultural needs of readers of *Scrutiny*, In an expanded version of the essay, *Scrutiny of Cinema*, Hunter – while identifying a handful of 'good' films - sees the vast majority as threatening - 'a new opium'.[35] The simplicity of language used in the new talkies distresses Hunter's literary sensibilities, claiming: 'Simplicity is admirable; but there is a difference between the simplicity of *The Songs of Innocence* and Basic English.'[36]

An adaptation, unlike 'pure cinema', is a dangerous thing: if we take Virginia Woolf seriously, it is a major player in the decline of cultural values and the levelling of classes. A survey in 1911 revealed that 78 per cent of audiences were indeed from the working classes, a figure that suggests that the middle classes were voting with their feet, refusing to morally or intellectually contaminate themselves by attending 'the pictures'.[37] While there were some who welcomed cinema's capacity to instruct 'the masses', 'filling their humdrum, hopeless and pitiable existence with joy',[38] many saw the evils outweighing any good. As Archibald Henderson tells George Bernard Shaw, the only way to fight them is to ridicule them.[39] His advice, unfortunately, backfires on himself; he fails to recognise how some film adaptations, like the working class they're identified with, can mount serious challenges to such uninterrogated assumptions. This attitude has dominated much thinking on adaptation in the twentieth century and says much about the putative alignment of 'art' with the bourgeoisie. Dogged by unfavourable comparisons of the film to the book, the field has received little recognition beyond unsupported dismissals. Graham Greene, a literary film enthusiast, as mentioned above, was one of the few to challenge this implicit association of popularity with vulgarity: 'The cinema has got to appeal to the millions; we have got to accept its popularity as a virtue, not turn away from it as a vice.'[40] But this view has remained in the minority for the best part of the twentieth century.

Similarly, going against the grain was André Bazin, who in the 1950s argued a case for 'mixed cinema', asserting that when 'the film-maker plans to treat the book as something different from a run-of-the-mill scenario, it is a little as if, in that moment, the whole of cinema is raised to the level of literature'.[41] The baton was passed to George Bluestone, who was the first to write a book-length study on the subject of the novel *on* film. But Bluestone's work conveys a palpable anxiety about the field in his references to adaptations as 'paraphrases' and 'mutations', possibly based on an inability to shake off an essential logocentricism. He is not quick to credit film's potential to take on new challenges. While he asserts the impossibility of translating Joyce or Proust to screen ('Proust and Joyce would seem as absurd on film as Chaplin would in print'),[42] he also voices a concern over the moral and political influence of cinema in his utter astonishment that the heartthrob Gary Cooper could be proposed, by his fans, as a possible candidate for Vice-President.[43] Bluestone betrays an assumption that money and art or politics and entertainment are incompatible; one wonders how he would react to a Ronald Reagan or an Arnold Schwarzenegger (possibly as proof, for some, that politics and entertainment *are* indeed contrary to each other). For Bluestone, the key to adaptation studies is to acknowledge the different formative principles of literature and film, not to regard them as the same. This approach subtly moves away from the 'not as good as the book' argument, while paradoxically restating the superiority of literature over film. In this, Bluestone, unwittingly, throws obstacles in the path of literature on screen studies by perpetuating assumptions that (1) a book is unproblematically better than a film, and (2) a film has the capacity (but not the right) to morally and politically sway its audience. Perhaps owing to the reservations of Bluestone and the earliest critics of the field, literature on screen emerged as a very exclusive club: popular literature, working-class literature, cartoons, television adaptations, need not apply. The field also broke away from theatre and poetry so that adaptations of the novel became a field in itself with theatre, especially Shakespeare on screen, seeming to have an autonomy of its own.[44]

It's not surprising that Shakespeare on film was the first to break the barrier into English Studies, as Shakespeare's name, associated, above all others, with value and respectability, serves to validate the study of 'mixed cinema'. But even Shakespeare on screen, as a sub-discipline, didn't really get going until the last decade of the twentieth century. Although there are a few surveys of Shakespeare films before this (Roger Manvell's *Shakespeare and the Film*, 1971 and Jack Jorgens's *Shakespeare on Film*, 1977), by the late 1980s, Shakespeare on screen had acquired respectability within most English departments, perhaps as a result of the decision to devote an entire issue of *Shakespeare Survey* (1987) to the topic. Co-edited by Anthony Davies and Shakespeare editor, Stanley Wells, the inclusion of analyses of Shakespeare on screen within a highly esteemed annual gave the green light to numerous books, articles and journals devoted to the subject during the 1990s: to list a few, Anthony Davies, *Filming Shakespeare's Plays* (1988); John Collick, *Shakespeare, Cinema and Society* (1989); Peter Donaldson, *Shakespearean Films/Shakespearean Directors* (1990); Lorne Buchman, *Still in Movement: Shakespeare on Screen* (1991) and Linda Boose and Richard Burt (eds), *Shakespeare the Movie* (1997). Up until 1997, you could count on one hand the number of books devoted to the subject each year, and after that, it's virtually impossible to keep track. Undoubtedly, Shakespeare on screen, in spite of a culture of anxiety regarding the impact of media studies on English literature, is here to stay,[45] but few of the commentaries in this area are concerned with scrutinizing approaches to adaptation as an object of study in its own right.

It's clear that the name 'Shakespeare' in 'Shakespeare on Screen' ensures a degree of academic credibility not always awarded other forms of cultural and/or film studies. While Shakespeare on screen seems to have been severed from adaptations studies on the whole, it does set the stage for canonical authors to receive a similar treatment. Next in line is Jane Austen, whose screened novels have begun to attract considerable attention, with collections, such as *Jane Austen in Hollywood* (ed. Linda Troost and Sayre Greenfield, 1998);

Recreating Jane Austen (John Wiltshire, 2001); *Jane Austen on Screen* (ed. Gina Macdonald and Andrew F. Macdonald) and Sue Parrill's *Jane Austen on Film and Television: A Critical Study of Adaptations* (2002); the growing interest in Austen's appropriation into popular culture is addressed by Kathryn Sutherland in *Jane Austen's Textual Lives: From Aeschylus to Bollywood* (Oxford: Oxford University Press, 2005). Resulting from the success of the BBC adaptation of *Pride and Prejudice* (1996), screenwriter Andrew Davies shows how in the case of classic television adaptations it is possible for the screenwriter to gain renown almost as an auteur. Successful adaptations generate successful published screenplays, such as Emma Thompson's for *Sense and Sensibility* (1996), and there is a whole industry involved in providing behind-the-scenes films of 'the making of' a favoured adaptation, as if our hunger to get to the bottom of the process of convergence knows no bounds. Volumes of critical readings are emerging on other canonical writers on screen, such as Dickens, the Brontës, Thomas Hardy and Graham Greene, and publishers are producing series devoted to writers on screen, which announce that one way to approach authors on film is by the sum of their adaptations.

Following from Bluestone's pioneering work, development in the field was patchy, and Robert B. Ray, at the end of the twentieth century, complained that the entrenched 'not as good as the book' approach rendered adaptations studies at a standstill.[46] The twenty-first century has seen more varied and productive studies, ranging from intertextual readings as in the work of Robert Stam,[47] where the film is seen as not clinging to a single ur-text, but as part of a continuing dialogical process with a range of other texts. Kamilla Elliott has located adaptations within a tradition of *ut pictura poesis*, dividing the field between inter-art affinities and inter-art analogies, while considering both sides of the relationship between film and literature: the harmonic and the antagonist.[48] This gradual acceptance of canonical literature on screen over the twentieth century is mirrored in reviews of adaptations over the century and changing attitudes of writers to adaptations of their works. If we take an adaptation of *Pride and Prejudice*, for instance, we can see a gradual softening and, indeed, a sea change in responses to the form. The 1940 film, starring Laurence Olivier and Greer Garson, received a very short acknowledgement in *The Times* with a slightly sniffy evaluation: 'The result is something that Mr. Bennett [*sic*] might have commended – somewhat coolly.'[49] This is in direct contrast to the 'Darcymania' following Andrew Davies's adaptation of 1995 and the numerous and excited reviews of the 2005 film, directed by Joe Wright. Adaptations are no longer referred back to the imagined disdain of the author of the originary text, and 'high literary' adaptations are, on the whole, welcomed by their critics as contributing to an ongoing dialogue about the author and their works. Reviewed in the *Guardian*, Wright's *Pride and Prejudice* is regarded as if it were a piece of literature itself: 'It is, as Hardy would put it, "majestic without severity, impressive without showiness, emphatic in its admonitions, grand in its simplicity".'[50]

The acceptance of literature on screen runs parallel with the emergence of the 'heritage' film, which strives to recapture and revere a historical period or a canonical literary text, to give the illusion that it has achieved what new historicist critic, Stephen Greenblatt, famously proclaimed to be his ambition – 'to speak to the dead'.[51] While, at long last, those involved in the production and reception of literature are taking adaptations of classic texts seriously, the field is still largely restricted to canonical writers, reinforcing and perpetuating Bluestone's seemingly paradoxical refusal to enter into unprofitable comparisons between book and film in which the book will always triumph over the film, while, at the same time, never looking beyond 'classic' literary texts, never entertaining the prospect that there are numerous types of adaptations and that adaptations can and do, in many instances, improve upon and move beyond their literary origins. There can be no doubting that the overt snobbery present in early discussions of the literary film still persists. Overall, the perspective of writers on film has been twofold: resentment for the torture and murder of the author, coupled with an essential logocentricism, entangled with elitism, which prioritises words over images and the middle class over the working class.

To return to more prosaic actualities, and as Joy Gould Boyum affirmed in 1985, 'the simple fact is that when a film is made of a novel, it tends to encourage reading rather than discourage it'.[52] Even if it is the case that the popular view of literary adaptations remains that 'whatever the quality of the original material, Hollywood's apprentice sorcerers are seldom credited with producing anything but "disappointing lead"',[53] film did not kill the 'classic' book but rather, via adaptations, assured it a stronger position within postmodern culture than it had achieved via high modernism. The modernists, with their ambiguous responses to film, revealed the deepest fears at the vanguard of high culture, yet as Brian McFarlane observes, recalling George Bluestone, 'paradoxically, the modern novel has not shown itself very adaptable to film'.[54] This situation is changing as it becomes clear that modernist adaptations are not technically impossible, or unthinkable, but require an audience that can move beyond invidious comparisons to the book and indulge their intertextual pleasures as much more sophisticated consumers of all contemporary cultural forms than critics often give them credit.

In contemporary adaptation criticism there is a great deal of analysis of the ways in which the film audience has grown and become more sophisticated since the days when untutored spectators shrieked in horror at the presumed disembodiment of actors in the process of a close-up. It is all the more surprising that even recent challenging criticisms of adaptations pay little attention to the relationship between spectating and reading in the twenty-first century, or of possible changes in our reading practices since the turn of the twentieth century and the shifting film audience, from predominantly working class to middle class. The model of reading presented tends to assume, even contrary to our better knowledge, that (a) we read prior to viewing an adaptation; (b) the 'imaginary *mise en scène*'[55] we might privately create as part of the process of reading is undisturbed by the imagination of others, besides film directors. This is partly disingenuous, figuring perhaps the critic as the model reader, since it is well known that an audience at a screening of a literary adaptation will comprise a substantial number who haven't read the novel in question, but may know much about it through various means. They may have a clear idea of, say, Austen's writing via countless other adaptations; they may be a student who, instead of reading the novel, chooses to glean what they can from an edition such as Cliff's Notes; they may have enjoyed an abridged version as a classic serial on the radio; they may have bought an audio version to listen to in their car; they may have read a long article about the book and its author. Even if they have bought the book, what publications emerge unheralded? What classic text comes to us without an ideological framework – if not the academic introduction that we may or may not read, then the cover design which acts as 'product placement' and tells us much about its relation to high or low culture? The dominance of the classic adaptation in discussion has prompted the creation of a model reader who fits a certain stereotype of high cultural activity – the person who reads, alone and respectfully from beginning to end. Perhaps our notion of film consumption remains a little behind the times as it is now, of course, equally the case that we don't always consume film in cinemas or other public places or even in one sitting (think of the amount of times one 'catches up' on recent films by getting the DVD on release or the way one might record older films for multiple viewing). The key point in all this is that we might get beyond some of the fundamental sticking points in adaptations criticism by not only refiguring the concept of the author's relationship to the text, but also that of reader or viewer.

One assumes that these 'savages' watching the pictures are unnerving to Woolf because she doesn't know if she understands the nature of their enjoyment, yet wants however to assume that it is primitive and uncomplicated. But what if the threat lies in the ability to absorb narrative in an unpredictable fashion? If the audience of a text is framed in such a way, one can open up Stam's notion of adaptation (following Genette and others) as an ongoing dialogical process:

> All texts are tissues of anonymous formulae, variations on those formulae, conscious and unconscious quotations, and conflations and inversions of other texts. In the broadest sense, intertextual dialogism refers to the infinite and open-ended possibilities generated by all the discursive practices of a culture, the entire matrix of communicative utterances within which the artistic text is situated, which reach the text not only through recognizable differences, but also through a subtle process of dissemination.[56]

According to Timothy Corrigan, 'adaptation today is not, as most commentaries would have it, primarily about textual integrity versus popularisation',[57] and he notes how authors rather than the text are 'returned' to latter-day adaptations of classic literature – most obviously in Patricia Rozema's *Mansfield Park* (1999), where extracts from Austen's own letters are used to refigure Fanny Price as the 'author' of *Mansfield Park*. For Corrigan, film audiences are far from passive and become, in fact 'participatory agents', closer perhaps to the notion of the active, historically framed reader of literature.

If we can rescue the film audience from the derisory view of them as primitive and helplessly duped and stupefied by the seduction of the image, we might also be better able to assess the fate of literature and film adaptations in the contemporary market-place. Looking back to our depiction of modernist writers' curiosity about film set against the dominant view of early cinema as created by 'artisans' rather than artists, appealing to the working class rather than the bourgeoisie, and ransomed to the demands of commerce and all its corrupting influences, we can recognise that economic factors, whether we like it or not, now embrace our consumption of culture, both high and low. Attempts to conceal the unpleasantness of the fusion of money with art has, in Jim Collins's view, produced the hybrid of 'high pop':

High-pop is, in large part, a reaction against the sordidness of aggressive mass marketing and blockbuster entertainment, yet its high-profile visibility depends on the incorporation of marketing techniques borrowed directly from that world. This has led to unprecedented developments in which institutions and tastes which were formerly thought to be mutually exclusive have become commonplace – *good design* chain stores, *blockbuster* museum shows, *high-concept* literary adaptations.[58]

Collins, in charting the shifting relationship between high art and popular culture, has shown that savages can all seek refinement at cost. The subsequent blurring of boundaries between literary and popular classifications, between 'high' and 'low' art forms, robs the century-long conflict between film and literature of some of its impact, and the changing academic spaces in which adaptations studies can flourish offer at least some counterpoint to Robert B. Ray's view that little 'distinguished work' on film and literature has been produced without the principal aim of confirming what novels can do that films can't. Ray is undoubtedly right in his assertion that the field of adaptation studies is dominated by the case study, but his conclusion that this allows for no metacritical perspective or that it inevitably is at the expense of film may be misguided. Adaptations critics know only too well how much easier it is to work through a critical position by the use of a key example, just as Barthes's *S/Z* would be the lesser theoretical text without its focus on *Sarrasine*. However, if we are all in agreement with the principle that every cultural artefact is an adaptation, this may unsettle how we view the boundaries of the field of *literary* adaptation. Indeed, for James Naremore, 'The study of adaptation needs to be united with the study of recycling, remaking, and every other form of retelling in the age of mechanical reproduction and electronic communication.'[59] In Ray's view, the perceived close link between film and literature is arbitrary; he suggests that cinema has just as much in common with architecture – 'both forms are public, collaborative, and above all, expensive',[60] arguing that unlike cinema and architecture, which both have to work within economic and other constraints, literary artists write what they please. Leaving aside the thorny question of whether literary artists, today or ever, write what they please, it is interesting to note that in making such a comparison Ray recalls the work of Vachel Lindsay, bringing us full circle to the earliest attempts to account for film's relationship to the literature it adapts. In the past it may have been the case that adaptation studies has been a field dominated by literary critics who use adaptation to shore up 'literature's crumbling walls',[61] but there is much evidence to suggest that adaptation studies has little care for the salvation of either literary or film studies.

In *A Theory of Adaptation*, Linda Hutcheon argues that the long-standing popularity of adaptations is due to the pleasure they generate in repetition and recollection. Using both the analogy of opera and Darwinian natural selection, she discusses 'classic' literature, popular forms and videogames, all under the umbrella of 'adaptation'. The attempt to answer what, who, why, how, and where coupled with the dizzying number of examples provided in the book point to the conclusion that there cannot be, as the title promises, *a* theory of adaptation. But this is both a weakness and the strength of the book that turns a corner in the field of adaptation by going beyond the elitist literary approaches that restricted literature on screen in the last century. Hutcheon appears to take the same position as Boyum when she asserts that an adaptation 'is not vampiric: it does not draw the lifeblood from its source and leave it dying or dead, nor is it paler than the adapted work. It may on the contrary keep that prior work alive, giving in an afterlife it would never have had otherwise.'[62]

Unlike Ray, we are more sanguine about the future of adaptations studies, and Linda Hutcheon shows us how far we have travelled since earlier pioneers of film criticism and in the seemingly infinite number and nature of relationships that literature can strike up with film, and vice versa. The study of adaptations, for Thomas Leitch, is the study of textualising, 'as the work-in-progress of institutional practices or rewriting'.[63] Early film critics, lacking a vocabulary to express the wonder of cinema or its potentialities, looked to the established arts for adequate conceptualisation; literary writers, meanwhile, were enticed by its form and repelled by the commercialisation of the industry and the 'quality' of the audience. Early adaptation critics were prompted to look at the relationship of literature to film because of the fact of adaptation as a key mode of narrative exchange in popular film, but their pioneering work has opened the way for us to speculate on notions of literary integrity, authorial identity and the real place of art in advanced global capitalism. We have tried to shed some of the class prejudices of our modernist forebears and celebrate the democratisation of 'art', an approach that can take us dangerously close to 'trash', in a heady whirl of high-pop cultural ambiguity.

4

Authorial Suicide: Adaptation as Appropriation in *Peter Pan*

This chapter explores a text that seems to have been conceived of and persists as an adaptation: *Peter Pan*. J.M. Barrie, best known for the authorship of *Peter Pan*, seems to have had a love/hate relationship with film adaptation, as testified in his own foray into the field with *The Real Thing at Last* (1916), an 'adaptation' of *Macbeth* which, as its title implies, lampoons film adaptation of literature for its inane belief in the superior 'reality' of the moving image. Barrie's many changes to the play, which was performed before Queen Mary, Princess Mary and Prince Albert, include the ending in which Macbeth and Macduff are joyfully reconciled, accompanied by a piano rendition of 'Life's Too Short to Quarrel'.[1] It seems that one of the points behind the production, as part of the Shakespeare tercentenary celebrations, was to protest that film adaptation of dramatic and literary work reduces everything to the same cinematic formula. But a survey of film adaptations of Barrie's most famous work reveals another story; each adaptation appropriates the text differently, translating it according to an ever-changing ideological, economic and social agenda.

Adaptation as appropriation is a study of audiences rather than authors, productions as ideologically rather than 'artistically' driven. Julie Sanders divides appropriations into 'embedded texts' and 'sustained appropriations', distinguished from adaptations as 'not always as clearly signaled or acknowledged as in the adaptive process'.[2] The *Oxford English Dictionary* defines 'appropriation' as 'the making of a thing private property, whether another's or (as now commonly) one's own; taking as one's own or to one's own use' and in a later, artistic context the word means 'The practice or technique of reworking the images or styles contained in earlier works of art, especially (in later use) in order to provoke critical re-evaluation of well-known pieces by presenting them in new contexts, or to challenge notions of individual creativity or authenticity in art.' 'Adaptation' is defined not as a take-over but as 'fitting, or suiting one thing to another'. 'Appropriation' can imply artificiality, possessiveness and violence, while 'adaptation', with its obvious Darwinian echoes, is natural and 'for the best'. For us, there is little if no distinction between an adaptation and appro-priation; the difference is only in the approach, an approach practised by cultural materialist criticism of Shakespeare and the Renaissance that emerged in the 1980s. Jonathan Dollimore defines the approach as an examination of ' "high" culture alongside work in popular cul-ture, in other media and from subordinated groups'; not pretending political neutrality (which is, of course impossible) it's an approach that views texts 'as inseparable from the conditions of their produc-tion and reception in history'.[3] Rather than examining 'Shakespeare', Graham Holderness considers the repackaging of Shakespeare within contexts of exploitation; as Holderness explains, instead of just ref-erencing 'the originating moment of production', 'analysis must con-cern itself not only with the contextual and contingent history bearing upon the originating moment of a text's production, but also with the subsequent history of that text's strategic mobilization and ideological incorporation by different cultural forces and different social forma-tions'.[4] Holderness's social and political readings of a text's afterlife, 'in a sense the only kind of life it ever has',[5] provide a model for the following analysis of the Peter Pan story.

Appropriation suggests the text is recycled property (where the word originates). It's not as if filmmakers are starved of material when they turn to a literary text as source for a film; there are distinct ideo-logical reasons for making such a choice. Christy Desmet and Robert Sawyer note that the word 'appropriation' means both a theft and a gift (allocation of resources);[6] the end product is a historically situ-ated commodity. If we look at the screen text as a commodity, then the focus is audience- rather than text-based. At the risk of oversimplify-ing, the two approaches can be distinguished insofar as, in common currency, 'adaptation' normally assumes the primacy of the literary text while 'appropriation' announces that the principal concern is with the audience.

In a sense, there is no definitive text for *Peter Pan* – from its very beginning it is, somewhat paradoxically, an adaptation. *Peter Pan* is also a striking case to chart as it has undergone countless adaptations, changing the story to appeal to different audiences; indeed, as mentioned above, it starts its life as an adaptation, as Barrie memorably reflected in his preface to the first published play text 24 years after its original performance: 'Some disquieting confessions must be made in printing at last the play of Peter Pan; that I have no recollection of having written it. Of that, however, anon. What I want to do first is to give Peter to the Five without whom he never would have existed.'[7]

Barrie suggests here that no ur-text exists – and that in the absence of one, he is providing us with a later version based on his recollections of what happened. The process of finally putting it to rest is articulated as painful – it is an announcement that it is over, that he must finally grow up and face the reality that the boys, that is, the five Llewelyn Davies boys that the author befriended and later adopted after the premature death of their parents, are now men. Indeed, the play was for Barrie just that, 'a play', a continuous game in which the story was constantly rewritten to take into account the present moment and the changing cast – whether it be the growing Llewelyn Davies clan, or the actors playing the Lost Boys, who each year had to be measured to see if they were still suitable for the role.[8] The story is a quintessential adaptation. Barrie seemed incapable of finishing *Peter Pan* and was constantly revising it to make it relevant to his audiences. His most famous change was to delete the line 'to die would be an awfully big adventure' when it was playing during the First World War to soldiers on leave, the war in which George Llewelyn Davies, the oldest of 'Barrie's boys', was killed.

The Dedication constantly alludes to the emergence of Peter Pan as a private game and it is framed as an intimate conversation to which the reader is an intruder: Barrie jocularly asks, 'What was it that made us eventually give to the public in the thin form of a play that which had been woven for ourselves alone?'[9] Not only is this dedication rendered all the more poignant because two of the boys, George and Michael, are by this time dead,[10] but it stands as his public denial of responsibility for the authorship of the story of Peter Pan. The boys are addressed in the present tense as if they were all still alive, and the passing of time is presented as if one could return and revisit the scene of these doings quite as easily as if the episodes were being staged as a play. The tone of this Dedication has all the playfulness of Barrie in his other prose works, and also suggests that it was Barrie's deepest wish to give back to the Llewelyn Davies children the aspects of their childhood games which inspired him to refine and retell the story so very often, even though for Peter Llewelyn Davies, popularly assumed by the audience to be the model for Peter Pan, it was 'that terrible master-piece'.[11] Barrie's narrative style here, as elsewhere, is characteristically intrusive and simultaneously self-effacing as he compiles the 'evidence' that he is indeed the author of *Peter Pan* – as if his implied reader (one of the boys, perhaps?) is calling this into question. This constant deferral of the origins of the story suits his purposes well, along with the staged 'appearance' of a statue of Peter in Kensington Gardens in 1912, seemingly spirited there at the dead of night. The status of Peter Pan as modern mythic hero is confirmed by his re-emergence in several forms and changing characteristics, but underpinned by key recurring themes – one being that he fled his nursery so that he did not have to grow up.

Originally written as a play in 1904, *Peter Pan*'s success was and is phenomenal. It is a story that is completely open to adaptation and its origins in drama particularly lend it to the medium of film. Not only did novelists feel threatened by the introduction of cinema; drama-tists as well were competing with this new and exciting medium, a medium that could do so much in such a short space of time and which threatened to steal their audiences. Much of the pleasure of watching Barrie's play derives from its defiance of the confines of the stage in its appropriation of cinema-like effects. The influence of cinema on Modernist literature is well known; but it's worth pausing and thinking that, in many ways, film provides not just an influence but, possibly, an ur-text for Peter Pan and much writing to follow.

Consequently, it's inevitable that the story of Peter Pan would become the topic of numerous screen adaptations, and as Andrew Birkin observes, Barrie lived to see 14 screen adaptations of his works[12] and was himself captivated by the possibilities of cinematography for the stage. Indeed, the early version of the story, *The Boy Castaways*, was an attempt at a graphic novel; Barrie's photographs of the boys were used alongside the narrative, suggesting Barrie's early interest in mixing media, and making literature visual. At one point, when Barrie was considering writing a revue for the actress Gaby Deslys, he planned to film guests at a banquet (Prime Minister Asquith included) to edit and project as a backdrop to her erotic dance routines.[13] What Barrie envisaged was a new marriage of theatre and cinema, though he was unable to realise this in his lifetime; and what is clear in later film adaptations of *Peter Pan* is the unique feature of his writing – the playful, cynical, sentimental and sometimes exasperating qualities of the narrative voice – is lost altogether.

As has been noted, Peter Pan, in many respects, could be seen to represent not only an expression of nostalgia for childhood, but also for a brother who died at a young age in a skating accident. Certainly for many, the idea of a forever young sibling would be common, given the numerous child fatalities in the Edwardian period, those who die young and therefore will be children forever. This image of 'lost' children echoes both the potentially brutal short lives of the young and offers an antidote to death itself while the lost boys remain on the island. In the novel they are described as 'the children who fall out of their perambulators when the nurse is looking the other way' by Peter; the explanation for why they are all boys is that 'girls, you know, are much too clever to fall out of their prams'.[14] Peter Pan first appeared in Barrie's novel, *The Little White Bird* (1902), where he was associated with death and was given the task of burying the dead children who break the rules and stay in Kensington Gardens after dark. Like Peter, dead children never grow older. The earlier novel is possibly recalled in the alarming description of the first sighting of Peter Pan by Mrs Darling; the window has blown open and something rushes in, disturbing the nursery: 'He was a lovely boy, clad in skeleton leaves and the juices that ooze out of trees; but the most entrancing thing about him was that he had all his first teeth. When he saw she was a grown-up, he gnashed the little pearls at her.'[15] At the time the play was written, one-quarter of children died before they reached the age of 5. Mrs Darling's fears are clearly of a disease, coming through the window and taking her children to their deaths. Indeed, Neverland is a place where death is a great adventure: as for the possibly endlessly multiplying lost boys, Peter 'thins them out'[16] in cold blood if they do not meet their death by adventure. Originally, it was Peter, not Hook, who was the villain of the piece – Hook was added in a later draft as the play was in preparation, becoming the evil father figure.

Initially the play called for a boy to play the part of Peter, but licensing laws in 1904 forbade this and therefore a woman, Nina Boucicault, was chosen as the first Peter. This is one of many accidental instances that became 'authoritative', and it has been the tradition to have Peter played by an adult woman up until about 20 years ago. In films this has been different, although the first version – the silent film of 1924 – cast a female in the part. In 1953, Walt Disney produced an animated *Peter Pan*. Changes were many, especially Tinker Bell, who, instead of a magical light, became a real figure, often thought to be modelled on Marilyn Monroe, but actually modelled on the pin-up girls of the Second World War, such as Betty Grable. The animated version was hugely influential in subsequent stage adaptations; and, although the novel and published play exist, albeit as adaptations themselves, they are not regarded as sacred texts in the way that 'Shakespeare', for example, can claim to be.

Peter Pan, 1953

Disney was very keen to get the rights to *Peter Pan* and the animated version proved the most popular yet. Disney's famous embracing of innocence in his films makes it immediately clear why he would be drawn to *Peter Pan*, which comes complete with its own 'magic kingdom': 'Innocence in Disney's world becomes the ideological vehicle through which history is both rewritten and purged of its seamy side.'[17] The first impression that we have of this post-Second World War production is that the violence is tamed down, the threat of death is removed and the focus is on domesticity and the differences between boys and girls, as well Europeans and 'natives'. Wendy is clearly linked with her mother – she visually replaces her on screen, and she has a maturity that is contrasted to the other children (with the exception of Peter), who are dressed in animal costumes, reflecting a need to be tamed by a mother. The sexualisation of Tinker Bell, together with a grown-up-looking Wendy (a mini Mrs Darling), function to endorse the desirability of growing up, to conforming to society's rules – particularly for girls. Wendy exists on the periphery of Neverland adventures – she is disliked by Tinker Bell, the bitchy mermaids and Tiger Lily, all who regard her as a sexual threat in Peter's regard for her. The implication is that friendship is a purely male domain. The women are stereotyped as either seductresses or mothers and Wendy's more wholesome charms win out over the scantily clad Tinker Bell and the mermaids.

In addition to the cult of domesticity, this film presents the natives of Neverland as unequivocal stereotypes. They are identified by the colour of their skin – in fact this is their sole identity. The genocide is described in the book as one great 'adventure', and this is reflected in the film by the replacement of a celebratory pow-wow. Unsurprisingly, the Indians are excised in Spielberg's *Hook,* alluded to possibly in the costumes of the Lost Boys, especially the leader, Rufio, whose skin and dress recall that of the original inhabitants of North America. In the 2002 *Return to Never Land* all that remains is a totem pole. Disney goes further than the novel in 1953 in his portrayal of the Indians, asking the question, 'what makes them red?'

Wendy, the quintessential English little lady, is appalled at the rituals of the Indians, which imply something more primitive than her own society. They are linked to the children and Wendy's disapproval of them is similar to her disapproval of the youngsters. Tiger Lily's kiss literally turns Peter Pan red – the blushing Peter provides the answer to the question of why is the Indian red. The red men and women are portrayed as if in a permanent state of sexual excitement (constantly blushing), and are thus more akin to animals than are the white Europeans.[18] The film perpetuates a myth that the Indians are inferior, as they exist on a lower physical plane – all but Tiger Lily are portrayed as corpulent and grotesque.

At the end of Barrie's novel, the travellers return to heartbroken parents, as if coming back from the dead, and they are able to literally turn the clocks back. Mr Darling also literally comes out of the doghouse and is restored to his family, and the Lost Boys are admitted into the Darling household. The boys all grow up and become ordinary adults. What is striking about the ending is how quickly time passes – compared to the timelessness of the Neverland, where no one grows old, here we have time passing at an alarmingly quick pace:

> As you look at Wendy you may see her hair becoming white, and her figure little again, for all this happened long ago. Jane is now a common grown-up with a daughter called Margaret; and every spring-cleaning time, except when he forgets, Peter comes for Margaret and takes her to the Neverland, where she tells him stories about himself; to which he listens eagerly. When Margaret grows up she will have a daughter, who is to be Peter's mother in turn; and thus it will go on, so long as children are gay and innocent and heartless.[19]

The final paragraph comes as a shock – the pace is so quick – the fear of growing up, implied throughout the narrative – is replaced with the harsh reality of time passing. The male-centred story has changed too – the focus is on Wendy, not Peter – possibly suggesting that while men stay the same, women are changing, developing at an alarming rate, and Peter has been left behind. The ending of the novel presents the future through the matriarchal line and this focus on the changing female might be accounted for by the changing position of women in society in the early twentieth century, in which Barrie was writing. Barrie is possibly suggesting that men are the ones who are fearful of change: so while the men remain Peter Pan-like, stubbornly the same, women are progressing, changing at an alarming rate. It is possible that central to the novel is the belief that a girl is 'more

use than twenty boys'.[20] Women's functional roles are portrayed as
overlaying their very individuality, whereas Peter and Hook, not to
mention all the lost boys, have their own histories, their own personal
explanations for how they came to be (for example, we're told about
Peter's mother and Hook's public school education). Lynda Haas
asserts that 'the mother and the mother–daughter relationship are,
as yet unsymbolised in our cultural imaginary. There is no maternal
genealogy, no importance attached to a mother's heritage.'[21] Whilst
Barrie figures precisely that – a maternal genealogy – at the end of the
novelisation of *Peter Pan*, the mother remains indeterminate, a girl's
destiny and the mark of maturity, whereas fathers have no such rite of
passage.

What surprises us about the Disney ending is the removal of the
parents' pain – they are not left for days without their children and
the fear of loss through death is entirely excised. Mr Darling isn't
in the doghouse, but is reconciled to the dog, and the Lost Boys do
not return with the children to the Darling household. The period,
renowned for its creation of the nuclear family, remains intact: two
parents, three children and a dog. Indeed it's almost as if the whole
thing was a dream; and Wendy and her father are totally reconciled –
she's prepared to grow up and he is prepared to accept her as she is.
Typically, the father has the final word in this – 'I think I saw that ship
a long time ago' – and with this clue that the father recalls his own
boyhood we are left with the feeling that patriarchy has been restored
and that the women are now in good hands.

Wendy is not replaced with Jane – her daughter – in this adaptation.
This Peter is a more romantic one than in Barrie's text and therefore
incapable of exchanging one Wendy for another one or forgetting
Tinker Bell. He still has his milk teeth in the novel, which would place
him around 6 years old – in Disney, he appears to be between 11 and
14, on the verge of sexual maturity. As the Barrie version flirts with a
matriarchal conclusion, the Disney version provides us with a decid-
edly patriarchal ending; everyone is reconciled to their position in society, just like Nana, who at the beginning of this film, hands Mr Darling
the rope, willingly allowing herself to be restrained. Indeed, the dog
is the moral centre of the film in its silent preaching of conformity
over rebellion and its celebration of a patriarchy to which everyone
willingly submits. Whereas in the novel, we have argued, patriarchy
is indeed at crisis point with Mr Darling being conveyed to and from
work in his kennel, as self-inflicted punishment for having made a mis-
judgement that placed his family in jeopardy.

Hook, 1991

While the Disney film preserves the period in which the book was written, *Hook* translates it to the late twentieth century – and this is, indeed a translation, rather than interpretation or preservation of the text. 'Updating' or 'modernising' the text entails a number of necessary changes – it would be no longer appropriate to refer to 'redskins' and the children can't be abandoned to the care of a dog in a live-action film. In fact, increased public awareness of paedophilia in the 1990s and beyond ensures that children would not allow themselves to be taken away by an intruder in the middle of the night. This is a period which saw reported an increasing number of child abductions – and this would be an ultimate taboo in a film directed at children. You can't have 1990s kids running away with an intruder who, in reality, is a very old man. As a consequence, these children have to be kidnapped – they don't go of their own volition. They are, however, like the children in the original story, insofar as they are displeased with their father – although he is not abusive, he is negligent. He has forgotten what it is like to be a child – in fact, he has forgotten that he is Peter Pan.

In *Hook*, we are told that Peter Pan saw Wendy's granddaughter and fell in love with her. Wendy arranged for him to be adopted by American parents so we have, in the Disney tradition, an American Peter Pan. And in the tradition of Disney (and many Hollywood movies), the good guys are the Americans and the bad guys – the pirates – are British. Purposefully, the American actor who plays Hook, Dustin Hoffman, adopts an English accent for the role. As in Disney's animation, London is viewed through the eyes of the (American) visitor with prominent signifiers of London – such as Big Ben, taxis, and the furniture and period of Wendy's house – giving us a clichéd tourist account of the city, just as Big Ben and Tower Bridge are used as key signifiers of London in the 1953 animation. In fact the house itself seems to be frozen in the past – the decor reflects a nostalgia for the past – but the past as it is re-created in the present. Rather than the first decade of the twentieth century, the house reflects the last decade of the twentieth century in the taste in Edwardian antiques, especially to do with children's toys, such as rocking horses, doll's houses and teddy bears. The appearance of an Edwardian-looking Wendy, played by Maggie Smith, and a late twentieth-century Peter, played by Robin Williams, reinforces the initial gap between then and now.

This film pays homage to Barrie's legacy rather than grasping for an 'original' amongst Barrie's own multiple Peters, and it uses both play and novel in addition to Disney for its sources: we are told, by Wendy, that the story was recorded by J.M. Barrie, who used to live next door to them. Indeed Wendy is honoured by Great Ormond Street Hospital, the hospital to which Barrie left the rights to *Peter Pan* and which still benefits from Barrie's profits; although expiring in 2007 in Europe, copyright lasts until 2023 in the United States.

The film's nostalgic strand is not just a hankering after the uncomplicated pleasures of childhood, but a nostalgia for the period in which the novel was set. The technological present, symbolised by Peter's brick-sized mobile phone, has overpowered the simpler, more rewarding pleasures of life, as reflected in a previous time. The children are linked with an earlier age to suggest that life was purer and simpler in the past and their leisure pursuits are traditional: Maggie is seen performing in the play *Peter Pan* (literally becoming her great-grandmother as the novel version foretells) and Jack takes part in a baseball game. Rather than a romantic association between Peter and Wendy, we have the 'family romance' where Peter Banning must rediscover his own origins in order to understand his actions as a father. The Neverland is a place where the family isn't forgotten, but remembered and restored: Tinker Bell (played by Julia Roberts) attempts a seduction, but gracefully gives way to the pulls of marital monogamy and parental responsibility. Maggie takes the place of Wendy; whereas in the Disney film she is a 'young lady', here she is clearly a little girl who learns to believe that Peter Pan is her father.

While Barrie's text challenges patriarchy and while Disney's film celebrates and affirms it, Steven Spielberg presents fatherhood in a more ambiguous light. Peter has become the bad father, the Mr Darling at the beginning; visually this is signalled at the end by his visiting the doghouse. This version owes as much to other 'parenting' films of the time as it does to Barrie's texts – best represented by *Baby Boom* (1987), where Diane Keaton plays a Yuppie who 'inherits' a small baby and tries to combine its care with big business, and ends up setting up her own home-based work, and *Parenthood* (1989), a rather mawkish Steve Martin comedy which follows the tribulations of three generations of one family, but focuses on one father's (Martin's) troubled relationship with his eldest son. *Hook* is also a parenthood text and Hook himself tries to usurp the fatherly role by telling Jack some home 'truths' such as 'Before you were born they were happier' and suggesting that parents only tell stories to send their children to sleep. Maggie, the daughter, is never beguiled by Hook and continuously identifies with her mother, becoming the 'mother' to the pirates when she sings. The struggle between Pan and Hook, therefore, becomes the struggle over the son and heir. Peter only recalls the times he has let his son down and it is only the father–son relationship that is portrayed as fraught with difficulties, as it is in all versions of the Peter Pan story, where fathers disappear or become emasculated.

Spielberg turns the story inside out by bringing Peter home, uniting father and son and changing the meaning of the text from 'to die would be an awfully big adventure' into 'to live would be an awfully big adventure'. The fear of death and the horrors of child mortality are removed entirely from the 1991 retelling of the story. As in the 1953 story, patriarchy has been restored and its crisis is resolved by Peter's reinvention of the role of father for the postmodern age.

Return to Never Land, 2002

Disney's 2002 sequel is, in common with most Disney sequels, partly a homage to the Disney 'original' as well as, more cannily, a vehicle by which to profit from the 'classic' status of the 1953 version which ties in with their habit of re-releasing well-loved films periodically, having created a demand for them. Unlike *Hook*, which signals a return to Barrie's novel version when the adult Peter finally remembers his past in order to reclaim the 'happy thought' that will enable him to fly ('I wanted to be a Daddy'), this sequel takes as its lead the closing passage of the novel and focuses on Wendy's daughter, Jane, during the period of the Second World War.

Jane is, significantly, the opposite of her mother, who still lives in the fantasy world of Neverland, telling endless stories to her small son Daniel. Jane, conversely, is a pragmatist, always armed with her notebooks and giving her younger brother a pair of socks for his birthday – a sensible wartime investment. Given that she takes no part in listening to her mother's stories, Neverland has to come to her, in the form of Hook's flying ship, last seen silhouetted against the moon and piloted by Pan in the 1953 version, but now manned by Hook and his crew, a sinister accompaniment to the planes and bombs surrounding her family. She is a heroine in the model of late twentieth-century Disney productions such as *The Little Mermaid* (1989), *Beauty and the Beast* (1991), *Pocohontas* (1995) and *Tarzan* (1999), who can fend for herself and is suitably scornful of Peter's rescue of her, denying kisses and refusing to be 'mother'. She is dressed in the prim nightdress that Wendy wore, but the outfit is completed by a pair of sloppy socks. Ultimately she will rescue Peter from Hook's clutches; but in some ways conforming to one abiding feminine stereotype of Eve, she will have been the potential source of his destruction, having initially entered into a pact with Hook. Even where this film overtly 'updates' the knee-jerk sexism of the 1953 version, particularly in Jane's claim to be the first 'lost girl', it re-enforces the social power of gender difference. The fact that she is a lost *girl* takes on an entirely different resonance: Jane has been made a 'grown-up' by the war and by her father's request that she look after Daniel and her mother while he goes into combat; more than that he has made her a 'man'. Perhaps her cynicism about fairies (which almost costs Tinker Bell her life) and Neverland pre-empts the feelings of the contemporary child viewer who, so often bombarded with the rawest images of current conflicts and atrocities, might feel the necessity to share Jane's cynicism. Jane's conversion gives them 'permission' to believe in fairies and to re-create a barrier between fantasy and reality, broken down by a decade and more of 'reality' television. On her return home she immediately embraces her brother and begins to tell him stories herself, taking on the mantle of 'mother' when she is released from her more 'masculine' role of head of the household as her father is seen returning from combat.

The placing of the events of this film at such an important modern historical juncture invites a more historicised reading of the film so that the timelessness of Neverland is more emphatically juxtaposed by the passing of time and its consequences. Just as Peter Banning is assailed by the trappings and responsibilities of modern life to the point that he has lost the simple pleasures, so Jane's journey to Neverland is undertaken on the eve of her and Daniel's planned evacuation into the country. The war is presented from a more child-centred view where the enemy is not portrayed, simply the effects of war, the bombing and destruction, air raids and scenes of children being shipped away from danger. Symbolically a possibly American revisionist view of the British role in the Second World War becomes dominant when Wendy tries to escape the island on a raft fashioned by herself and decked out with a Union Jack, only to sink ignominiously to the strains of 'Rule Britannia'.

The moral of the story, as in *Hook*, tells us that we, as adults, are in danger of becoming 'lost boys' insofar as we have forgotten what it is like to be a child. Jane, the sceptic because of her wartime experiences, mirrors today's children, inured to the harsh realities of both postmodern war and the intrusive and voyeuristic treatment of all tragedy, and therefore unable to enjoy fantasy. Disney, it is suggested, still holds the keys to the magic kingdom and children's imaginations.

Peter Pan, 2003

Directed by P.J. Hogan, the next adaptation capitalizes on the late twentieth, early twenty-first century's popular rite-of-passage narratives (most noticeably, the Harry Potter stories and Philip Pullman's *His Dark Materials*), transforming Peter and Wendy into prepubescent teenagers (we're told by Mrs Darling that Wendy is 'not yet 13'). While claiming to be the first live-action mainstream film adaptation of Barrie's story, Hogan's *Peter Pan* is as much an adaptation of other popular early teen television programmes and films; as one cynical reviewer in *Eye Weekly* noted, there's an uncanny resemblance between Wendy's brothers and Harry Potter and Ron Weasley,[22] reflecting an irresistible desire to cash in on a successful recipe. This version is framed by the kiss – the real kiss that Wendy gives Peter energises him into the ultimate defeat of Captain Hook. Like the previous adaptation, Wendy is given more of an active role, as she is an accomplished swordfighter and an aspiring novelist who ultimately becomes a successful writer, as is implicit in her grown-up narration of the film. The film is replete with scenes of Peter and Wendy looking at each other through various framing devices, such as the heart-shaped patterns on the bed in Wendy's nursery; the focus on the bedroom at the beginning of the film draws on the genre of the teen-pic, in which girls' rooms are focal sites. In keeping with popular children's literature of the turn of the century, this is a darker version than previous cinematic adaptations, with Hook routinely killing a pirate in virtually every scene in which he appears. The association of the narrative as memorial, or Peter as a dead child who will never grow up, is perhaps why Mohamed Al-Fayed chose to back the movie and why it is dedicated to the memory of his son, Dodi Al-Fayed, who was killed with Princess Diana in a car crash in 1997 (Dodi Al-Fayed was also executive producer for *Hook*). Hogan's film repeatedly pays homage to Disney, opening, as in the 1953 adaptation, with an animated version of London, directing our gaze into the window of the Bloomsbury house. As in the Disney film, Mr Darling wants Wendy to move out of the nursery, and his reconciliation with her provides the emotional climax at the end of the film. This film includes two kisses which blatantly reference the one kiss in the Disney film, where the kiss is associated with the 'red skins' of the native Americans (the blushing complexion which associates them with a constant state of sexual arousal); Tiger Lily kisses John, who turns an artificial red, and Wendy kisses Peter, who turns pink, further underlined by Captain Hook crying, 'You've turned pink Peter, you've turned pink!' Nana and the children's first excursion out of the nursery is to Mr Darling's bank, where the upheaval caused is visually reminiscent of *Mary Poppins*, reinforced by the opening of numerous umbrellas at the close of the sequence. Echoing Peter Banning from *Hook*, this Peter rewrites Barrie's words at the end of the film with 'To live would be an awfully big adventure.'

Visually Peter bears the hallmark of the 1953 Disney film, which seems to have permanently anchored the image of Peter into a wily figure with dishevelled hair, dressed in a tight-fitting tunic, with hands almost perpetually on hips. However, Mr Darling, in this version, has been changed. Not only are we returned to the theatrical precedent of having both Mr Darling and Hook played by the same actor (in this case Jason Isaacs), but he bears a distinct resemblance to J.M. Barrie himself, both physically and in his quirky, stifled playfulness. The omitted scenes with Darling in the doghouse make this connection all the more obvious, recalling photographs of the serious, gaunt, conservatively dressed author virtually dwarfed by his own Newfoundland dog. The film doesn't shirk from the violence of the story but is clearly uneasy with the figure of Mr Darling, choosing to close down any explicit association between the father and the author, rather than addressing it head on.

Finding Neverland, 2004

Becoming a father is, in essence, the thematic thrust of the next 'Peter Pan' adaptation, Marc Forster's biopic of Barrie, *Finding Neverland*, starring Johnny Depp and Kate Winslet and based on the play *The Man Who Was J.M. Barrie* by Allan Knee. In this film, Barrie's creativity is fuelled by his unspoken and tragic love for Sylvia Llewelyn Davies and his increasingly paternalistic feeling for her four sons (the youngest son, Nico, who would still be a baby, was removed from the film in order to make the boy's father's death less recent). The film is interspersed with grand, theatrical occasions, commencing with an opening night in 1903 of a little known play by Barrie (*Little Mary*), which, for a contemporary audience, has all the features of a glamorous Hollywood premiere, with beautifully dressed famous faces walking along the red carpet into the theatre. Revealingly, the sequence is first identified, in the Director's Commentary, as a movie premiere, unwittingly, perhaps, indicating that one of the subtexts of the movie is to portray theatre as increasingly filmic, culminating in the final 'theatrical sequence' in which the production of *Peter Pan* generously brought to Sylvia on her deathbed is transformed into what can only be described as a cinematic experience. Barrie's play has the power to entrance even the, up until now, disapproving, crusty mother of Sylvia, played by Julie Christie (who leads the audience in clapping during the 'Do you believe in fairies' sequence), and as the play unfolds, the wall of the theatre is lifted and the enraptured audience experience Neverland in a way that is only possible through cinema. The most memorable (or forgettable) moment of the movie is when the dying Sylvia walks through the wall and joins the inhabitants of Neverland. Nonetheless, this privileging of cinema over theatre shows the confidence, if not arrogance, of twenty-first-century literary adaptations, intimating film's audacious triumph over death in the immortalising of Sylvia, permanently transplanted onto a film set of Neverland. The film is punctuated by a play or games becoming, to use Barrie's words, 'the real thing at last';[23] the viewer is transported from stilted, highly artificial sets to a range of film genres, from the musical (Depp dancing with a bear surrounded by clowns), the pirate adventure and the Western. In this film, the play is repeatedly metamorphosed into a film and it is the 'film' rather than theatre which engages our emotional responses – although sometimes these responses may not be those intended by the director.

The film makes little effort at historical accuracy; according to the Director's Commentary, to be deprived of your own creativity and inspiration would be a crime in a film that celebrates both of these. Barrie is remoulded into a man who appeals to a twenty-first-century audience: he is a celebrity akin to the actor, Johnny Depp, who plays him. (Latterly, the connection between Barrie and Depp has been strengthened by his £1 million donation to Great Ormond Street Hospital in 2008 after his daughter was treated there while suffering a critical illness: he secretly visited and read to sick children whilst dressed in his Jack Sparrow costume). While the *Times* reviewer finds it 'difficult to work out just who the charming but rather idiosyncratic *Finding Neverland* is aimed at',[24] this is very much a film of its time aimed, we would argue, at an audience intrigued by celebrity culture, especially Johnny Depp fans, who are treated with revivals of Depp as Pirate Jack Sparrow, Winslet, as ill-fated lover (*Titanic*) and Dustin Hoffman, returning to Peter Pan after *Hook*. The film is framed by the big premiere, evoking Hollywood glamour and the magical trans-formative and, in this film, redemptive nature of cinema itself.

Significantly, each text that we've looked at has constructed chil-dren, race, gender and nationalism differently. We have suggested that the novel, unlike the film adaptations, is a critique of timelessness, as evidenced in the absurdity of Peter standing still while Wendy becomes an important part of the historical process. Through the novel we can call into question the position of women, the massacre of the indig-enous population of the island, and the class system (the nurse is not only treated like a dog; she is a dog).

All of these adaptations display their own historical periods boldly. Disney, whose stories favour harmony and closure, shuns the starkness of the ending of Barrie's play and novelisation with its melancholy message of death and forgetfulness. In each of the Disney cartoon ver-sions it is the mother who is first greeted on the children's return, and yet the narrative is not complete until the father returns to the heart of his family. In the 1953 version he is made to see sense and recognise that the nursery is women's (or females' – women and dogs') domain. In the 2002 version the return of the father does not just suggest famil-ial but also national cohesion in its implication that the war is coming to an end. Neither father is shown to self-consciously interrogate what fatherhood might mean when motherhood is so obviously symboli-cally attached to biology and nature, but *Hook*'s Peter does. Set in a period when anxiety increases over the role of parenting, because so much social dysfunction is attributed to upbringing, and in a period that makes much of sexual equality ('parenting' as opposed to 'mother-hood' and 'fatherhood'), Williams's portrayal of Peter is of a man in crisis. Like the men, bewildered by feminism who sought their primi-tive selves through movements such as Robert Bly's 'Iron John', Peter Banning returns to his boyhood self only to discover what made him want to grow up. His desire for Wendy's granddaughter Moira is fig-ured as the desire for children; and the conception of the family is cleansed of all the sexual complexities identified by Freud at the time Barrie's play emerged. In each adaptation subsequent to the play and novel, it is the family itself that represents timelessness: a concept cleansed of history, ideology and social dysfunction.

5

Beyond Fidelity: Transtextual Approaches

Film reviewers today are often unconcerned as to whether a film adaptation is 'faithful' to its literary source, in the sense of attention to detail and inclusiveness. Rather than what's left out, more attention is cast on what is added; it is the additions, not the deletions to the source that are largely responsible for an adaptation's box-office and critical success. To take Shakespeare as an example, Kenneth Branagh's carrying of a dead child across the bloody battlefield of Agincourt in *Henry V* (1989), Baz Luhrmann's use of guns for swords in *William Shakespeare's Romeo + Juliet* (1996), the flashbacks in Branagh's adaptation of the complete 1623 text of *Hamlet* (1996), and the use of Blockbuster's video store in Michael Almereyda's *Hamlet* (2000) were applauded as defining moments in these films. It was the liberties taken or the intertexts of the films rather than 'faithfulness' that were admired. This was not the case in the early Harry Potter films. Criticism was dominated by 'the not as good as the book' argument and the changes that were made were greeted with outrage. Taking a close scrutiny of the first in the series, *Harry Potter and the Philosopher's Stone*, we will try to account for the seemingly anachronistic reviews of Chris Columbus's first Harry Potter film.[1]

The consensus view seems to have been that, although financially successful, the film fails as an adaptation as it cannot compete with the book. In this section, we suggest that so-called 'faithful' adaptations are bound to disappoint, whereas reading intertextually or dialogically can, as Robert Stam has indicated, 'help us transcend the aporias of "fidelity" and of a dyadic source/adaptation model which excludes not only all sorts of supplementary texts but also the dialogical response of the reader/spectator'.[2] Stam uses Gérard Genette's concept of 'transtextuality', drawing on Julia Kristeva's concept of intertextuality and Mikhail Bakhtin's notion of dialogism, defined by Stam in the service of adaptation as 'the infinite and open-ended possibilities generated by all the discursive practices of a culture, the matrix of communicative utterances which "reach" the text not only through recognizable citations but also through a subtle process of indirect textual relays'.[3] Relying on Stam's model, this section reflects on the pros of reading adaptations intertextually or 'transtextually' and the cons of reading 'faithfully'. Genette's five transtextual relations are:

1 intertextuality – largely generic allusion and references in texts
2 paratextuality – the surroundings of a book or film (DVD featurettes, excluded scenes, titles)
3 metatextuality – the commentary on the 'source' text and on the adaptive process
4 architextuality – where an adaptation is structurally connected to a source text
5 hypertextuality – one text's (hypertext's) relation to another (hypotext). Stam refers to adaptations as hypertexts originating in hypotexts. Numerous adaptations (a high degree of hypertextuality) can confirm or reflect the canonical status on the hypotext.[4]

Undoubtedly, the announcement of the film, *Harry Potter and the Sorcerer's Stone* (controversially, 'Philosopher' was changed to 'Sorcerer' in order to accommodate the tastes and understanding of an American audience) boosted sales of the book – the books became, and still are, bestsellers, indeed the best-selling children's books of all time, exceeding the sales figures of Roald Dahl (who, in turn, overtook Enid Blyton as the most popular children's writer). The trailer (one of the film's many paratexts) took its inspiration from Disney, with the caption 'Let the magic begin', whetting expectations that the film would be even better than the book, and reminding us that the magic the book asks us to imagine can be realised by the technological possibilities of film. Film adaptations of children's literature often begin with a picture of a book opening into a 'real' world, implying that the film of the book will be an infinitely superior experience to that of its literary source. Viewers reared on Disney will instantly recall the figure of Tinker Bell who prefaces a movie by sprinkling fairy dust from her wand, dissolving the credits on the screen. The implicit message introducing the films is that the adaptation will be magical, vastly superior to its literary source which is, after all, only words.

But the film didn't transform the words into magic in the case of *Harry Potter and the Sorcerer's Stone* (Columbus 2001) or, indeed, in *The Chamber of Secrets* (Columbus 2002), which due to the disappointment generated by the first film, had lesser expectations thrust upon it. What was originally a brilliant marketing strategy backfired. Albeit a commercially successful film, in no way was it seen as coming close to the experience of the book, and the reasons for this are various. J.K. Rowling's involvement in the production (especially her insistence that the cast be British) and Columbus's attempt to keep as much of the book (in terms of range of scenes and incident) in as possible, extending the length of the film in order to ensure coverage of the text, ostracised audiences. In fact Columbus produced a far too faithful reading of the book to the point that, as Philip Nel reflects, 'watching *Harry Potter and the Sorcerer's Stone* is like watching a historical reenactment',[5] incapable of provoking the passionate responses inspired by the original. According to Adrian Hennigan, Columbus treated 'J.K. Rowling's debut novel with a reverence that wasn't even accorded to the Bible',[6] but in spite of this attention to detail, fans of the book were bound to see it as merely a pale copy of the original. The Internet Movie Database user's page is dominated by this view. One fan speaks for many when he says:

> This movie was incredibly good in its own sense, but being a complete nerd about these books, I have to say that the movie is woefully inadequate. Daniel Radcliffe seems too wimpy for Harry Potter. He should be a little awkward but in this movie he's a complete pansy. All in all, it was a pretty good book to movie transition but it was not anywhere near as good as *The Fellowship of the Ring*.[7]

In short, it was a film that tried too hard to *be* the book and one which was destined to suffer invidious comparisons with a much more successful book-to-film adaptation in the form of *The Fellowship of the Ring* (2001). If we look closely at the Harry Potter books and try to account for their extraordinary commercial success, it appears that they have been marketed and constructed as if *they* were the films. Inevitably, one triumphs and the other suffers from this confusion of identity.

Paratexts in the form of spin-offs, which John-the-Baptist-like come out prior to the film, were in the market-place about six months before the movie's release – these ranged from bookends, cuddly Norberts and Hedwigs, to copies of Bertie Bott's Every Flavour Beans. Although successful in marketing and generating income for the film, they also did the same for the book – possibly even more. In fact, it's easy to compare the marketing of the fourth instalment in the Harry Potter series, *Harry Potter and the Goblet of Fire* (released on 8 July 2000), to that of a film. The release of the fourth book was unashamedly promoted according to all the rules of Hollywood blockbusters, especially ones that herald a series of films, like *Jaws* (1975), *Star Wars* (1977) or *The Lord of the Rings* (2001). The release-day was announced months before and was celebrated with queues of customers waiting through the night, hundreds of adults and children attending bookshop events in order to collect their pre-ordered volume. The point that the marketing of the book followed closely the practices of Hollywood is an obvious one; but what isn't so obvious is that if we look in detail at the construction of the books themselves, even the very first book in the series, we can see how the writing itself adheres closely to the conventions of Hollywood. Perhaps this is the reason why the film adaptations disappointed so many viewers – that is the films don't fulfil the cinematic potential of the books, on a number of levels. The novels' appeal can be partially explained through Rowling's utilisation of a comforting and well-known formula, creating what can be defined as a new genre of Hollywood fiction. Moreover, the Hollywood-factor of the books is perhaps the major objection to them raised by the 'serious' critics. Anthony Holden, for example, rages: 'Harry Potter is an activity marginally less testing than watching *Neighbours*. And that, at least is vaguely about real life. These are one-dimensional children's books, Disney cartoons written in words, no more.'[8] Holden's assumption, that if it's like Disney, then it must be of no cultural value, is left uninterrogated, and the underlying message here is that the novels are too much like films –popular films at that – to be of any literary merit. Like many, he expresses distaste at the way in which an already successful series is marketed ever more fiercely with the appearance of each new volume in ways designed to establish status of this unique phenomenon – where each volume practically becomes a popular classic on the day of its publication. As noted, the film adaptation, *The Fellowship of the Ring,* eclipsed *Harry Potter and the Sorcerer's Stone*, inspiring observations such as Brian M. Carney's editorial in the *Wall Street Journal* (30 November 2001) entitled 'The Battle of the Books: No Contest. Tolkien Runs Rings around Potter'.[9] *The Lord of the Rings* was a better film because it adapted the novel to Hollywood conventions while, due to its huge band of young and loyal readers,

Columbus felt the need to preserve the book as much as possible – despite the clear impossibility of this aim. While the novels are full of references to books and reading, they also scrupulously adhere to the rules of classical Hollywood. Unofficially, these 'rules' consist of the prioritising of narrative over form, the use of little moral or narrative ambiguity, character-driven stories, the employment of generic structures (Horror, Gangster, Western, for example), secure space and time, a camera that is motivated by the needs of the characters, the assumption of a global audience between the ages of 16 and 24, inclusion of at least one action sequence, and an increasing addition of layers of self-reflexivity, involving quotations to other films.[10]

Harry Potter is, for better or worse, close to Anthony Holden's condemnation of it as 'Disney cartoons written in words' insofar as it precisely conforms to our cinematic expectations, especially the blockbuster (in its division into parts). Like a classical Hollywood film, the narrative is character driven, it has little moral ambiguity with a definite beginning middle and end and it's organised around the genre of fantasy/detective. The narrative is visually drawn with an emphasis on spectatorship throughout– for instance, Harry's passage to Platform 9¾ is quintessentially cinematic. This is a moment, like so many in the novels, that recalls the experience of watching a film. Like the movement from Kansas to Oz, one world instantaneously replaces another – Harry closes his eyes and opens them and we experience something like a dissolve in a film.

> – leaning forward on his trolley he broke into a heavy run – the barrier was coming nearer and nearer – he wouldn't be able to stop – the trolley was out of control – he was a foot away – he closed his eyes ready for the crash –
> It didn't come ... he kept on running ... he opened his eyes.
> A scarlet steam engine was waiting next to a platform packed with people. A sign overhead said *Hogwarts Express, 11 o'clock.* Harry looked behind him and saw a wrought-iron archway where the ticket box had been, with the words *Platform Nine and Three-Quarters* on it. He had done it.[11]

The Sorting Hat sequence borrows from the technique of flash cutting. Harry sees students 'craning to get a good look at him. Next second he was looking at the black inside of the hat.'[12] After a minute or two, the hat is off and vision is blurred as Harry slowly comes to his senses, where he finally 'could see the High Table properly now';[13] and the sequence culminates in a long shot. Rowling repeatedly returns to the climactic dissolve – a fade-out becoming a fade-in (famously utilised in Dorothy's departure from Oz and return to Kansas) – and these are most prominent at the climactic moments of the novel. Harry's final moments of consciousness, during death-defying heroics, are followed by an awakening into another world, introduced through blurred focus and a close-up shot of Dumbledore's glasses:

> He felt Quirrell's arm wrenched from his grasp, knew all was lost, and fell into blackness, down ... down ... down ...
>
> *
>
> Something gold was glinting just above him. The Snitch! He tried to catch it, but his arms were too heavy.
> He blinked. It wasn't the Snitch at all. It was a pair of glasses. How strange. ...
> 'Good afternoon, Harry', said Dumbledore.[14]

Other instances of intertextual references to the 'standard' Hollywood film include action sequences, such as the roller-coaster-like ride through Gringotts, the defeat of the troll and the journey through the trap door, punctuating the narrative in precisely the way they would be expected to in a film. Throughout the book there is an emphasis on the eyes: note, for example, the shifting points of view depending on who controls the gaze in the Mirror of Erised scenes, and Rowling is constantly calling attention to Harry's glasses, which function like the lens of a camera. Typical of Hollywood action movies, at the climactic moment of the book, the villain cannot resist explaining to his victim how his criminality evolved, enabling the hero time to be rescued (curiously, Quirrell's explanation is abbreviated in the film):

> It was Quirrell.
> '*You!*' gasped Harry. ...
> 'Me,' he said calmly. 'I wondered whether I'd be meeting you here, Potter.'
> 'But I thought – Snape –'[15]

Five pages of explanation follow, providing us with time for the rescue of Harry and Hollywood-style narrative closure.

At each level, the Harry Potter novels accord with classical Hollywood norms that have remained surprisingly fixed until the huge box-office successes of *Jaws* (1975) and *Star Wars* (1977), films that revolutionised Hollywood.[16] These new blockbusters produced a dazzling array of paratextual materials, including board games, computer games and a vast number of toys.[17] Included in these spin-offs are movie tie-ins and novelisations, and due to their explicit consumerism, they are largely dismissed by literary critics as cheap and trivial, only really serving to redirect our attention to the superiority of the film. It has been suggested that a common feature of postmodern Hollywood cinema is its intertextuality, which most often takes the form of referencing other films, perhaps, most frequently, *Star Wars*, in homage to that film's enormous impact on the film industry. In fact, Richard Keller Simon has gone so far to suggest that *Star Wars* has replaced the Bible as the ur-text of our civilisation,[18] and it undoubtedly provides a template for postmodern cinema, although a reference point that may now be lost on a new generation of cinemagoers.

In keeping with the current penchant for intertextuality in postmodern Hollywood, *Harry Potter* combines influences of and echoes to numerous other children's texts – among them *Cinderella, Lord of the Rings, Alice In Wonderland*, the Narnia novels, *The Famous Five, Just William*, the *Earthsea* sequence, *The Worst Witch, Matilda* and *The BFG*. Additionally, it recalls the experiences of films, such as *Superman* (with Harry as Clark Kent), and theme-park rides – the ride through Gringotts draws on our experience of roller-coasters, for example – as well as being so reminiscent of a similar scene in *Indiana Jones and the Temple of Doom* (1984). The pleasure of reading depends upon the recollection of numerous experiences, ranging from the sublime to the ridiculous. In fact, the story of Harry Potter is based as much on *Star Wars* as it is on any other text. As the first film trilogy – which can be regarded as the 'hypotext' of *Harry Potter* – centres largely round Luke's enigmatic relationship to Darth Vader, so too, Harry is incrementally associated with Voldemort, the 'dark father' of Rowling's series. Like Luke, Harry finds that he belongs to another world and that he possesses a force that makes him unique. Both texts feature two males and a female taking it upon themselves to fight against those who have gone over to the dark side. Voldemort betrays his teacher, Dumbledore, as Darth Vader did his master, Ben Obi-Wan Kenobi. As in the Arthurian legend, the weapon chooses its hero. Both Luke and Harry receive wands – Luke's originally belonged to his father, Darth Vader, whereas Harry's has sinister similarities to that belonging to Voldemort. Indeed, in both *Star Wars* and *Harry Potter*, the function of duelling (especially in matches between the dark father and the saviour/son) becomes incrementally important to the narrative – and whatever the superhuman properties of their weapons, the superior moral qualities of the hero are always emphasised in acts requiring real physical endurance and mental fortitude. It goes without saying that these duels take on phallic undertones as wands or light sabres are brandished: after all, these conflicts reinforce patriarchal

order – whether good or bad – and for many this seemingly unques-
tioned acceptance of male hegemony has caused some to see Rowling's
texts as essentially conservative.

Action sequences in both texts bear striking similarities – the passage through the trapdoor into the garbage compactor in *Star Wars*
(where unexplained foul creatures threaten below the surface) is
recalled in the journey through the trapdoor to the Devil's Snare in
Harry Potter. In both a seemingly soft landing is transformed into a
nightmare. Rowling's description of this instant reversal of fortune is
undeniably cinematic:

> 'We must be miles under the school,' [Hermione] said.
> 'Lucky this plant thing's here, really,' said Ron.
> '*Lucky!*' shrieked Hermione. 'Look at you both!'
> She leapt up and struggled towards a damp wall. She had to struggle
> because the moment she had landed, the plant had started to twist snake-
> like tendrils around her ankles. As for Harry and Ron, their legs had already
> been bound tightly in long creepers without their noticing.
> Hermione had managed to free herself before the plant got a firm grip
> on her. Now she watched in horror as the two boys fought to pull the plant
> off them, but the more they strained against it, the tighter and faster the
> plant would around them.[19]

Compare the above passage with the episode in *Star Wars IV* where
Luke Skywalker, Princess Leia and Han Solo are trapped in a garbage compactor. Quotations to the film can be found in the entrance
of Hagrid into the hut in the middle of nowhere (recalling the first
appearance of the morally ambiguous Darth Vader of Star Wars):

> SMASH!
> The door was hit with such force that it swung clean off its hinges and
> with a deafening crash landed flat on the floor.
> A giant of a man was standing in the doorway. His face was almost com-
> pletely hidden …[20]

And Harry's first visit to the Leaky Cauldron[21] prompts associations
with the tavern in *Star Wars*, inhabited by an array of exotic extra-
terrestrials, where Ben Obi-Wan Kenobi and Luke Skywalker eventually find Han Solo.[22]

The books are at their best as popular cultural artefacts when they
reread the defining popular texts of a previous generation (the parents
of the children who have contributed to the Harry Potter phenomenon)
and produce something which appears new and groundbreaking to

the next generation. There is no doubt that this generation of children growing up in the late 1990s and the first decade of the twenty-first century will be as much defined by memories of the Harry Potter novel sequence and all the debates it yielded about literacy and the return of reading, as they will by the key film texts such as *Lord of the Rings*. The films of Harry Potter novels can only offer us a pale imitation of the fiction and merely serve as some of the more pleasurable merchandising products that such a phenomenon demands, not least because the books had seemingly appropriated every marketing ploy available before a single film was released. This is very much to do with the films' perceived subservience to the novels and their author (and how many directors could boast the notoriety or mystique of J.K. Rowling?), but also much to do with the inevitable effects of filming fantasy literature. As Suman Gupta observes in *Re-reading Harry Potter*, 'The precondition of the making and reception of the *Harry Potter* films was their ability to provide a convincing *illusion of reality* of the Magic World, and they were to be tested and judged accordingly.'[23] To realise the magical effects of the books is to some extent to render them real and to necessarily conflate the worlds of wizards and Muggles – particularly since the Muggle world is a reflection on present-day middle Britain. As sophisticated film viewers, we would expect to be convinced by the special effects used to convey what are magical effects in the novels, and therefore to a large extent the film can only live up to our minimal expectations in this respect. Given that the books' existence as a phenomenon to be marvelled at, picked over, critiqued, but ultimately preserved delimits the importance of fidelity at the expense of the interpretive skills of the director; it can only fail to dazzle or amaze, but rather must know its subordination to the written word. The Harry Potter audience is not ready for a radical critique of the novels and their historical context is still too fresh for wide-scale cultural criticism, so that film adaptation as critical review is not an option and, given that the characters and stories are trademarked in both media, may never be.

It seems odd to enumerate the ways in which the *Harry Potter* sequence has prompted anxious debates about the possible return to primacy of the written word, but as Andrew Black notes, Harry Potter is a '*retrolutionary,* a symbolic figure of the past-in-future England which is in desperate need of such symbols'.[24] The Harry Potter novels nostalgically celebrate a reimagination of the past in the present by creating a fantasy world where quills and parchment are the key tools for getting on in the wizarding education system, but as fantasy these representations reside easily with the postmodern context in which readers absorb these texts. In the film versions, such artefacts live again in a conditional present, because the present tense is the key film tense, and their revival is portrayed without comment or awareness of the disharmony of such features. The books can provide all kinds of intertextual nostalgia for a readership whose access to the past may be mainly through fictional texts such as those by Blyton, Dahl or Barrie, but the films bring this to the present and produce something anachronistic and clumsy. The boarding-school environment in the novels adds symbolic dimensions to Harry's lack of family support or emotional location; in the films Hogwarts is an unpleasant reminder of the social entrapment of this generation of children, never likely to know the pleasures of playing in the local park without parental supervision, but having to accept that the 'forbidden forest' is forbidden for quite pragmatic reasons. At another level the Hogwarts environment is infinitely seductive and in the film the boarding-school setting comes across as quintessentially English – the boarding-school story having been a staple of previous generations of children's fiction and made familiar to thousands of children never likely to experience such an education or its incumbent privileges, through the works of Blyton and others. The imagery of the boarding school and the fantasy of being the orphaned child with as yet undiscovered magical powers speak to some of the most profound fantasies of children who feel free to imagine a space without parental control, and with the superhuman strengths to repel the efforts of those who wish children harm. In the film version, magic must be portrayed with equal commitment to realism as the dull predictability of Privet Drive, with some perverse effects whereby Hogwarts seems the duller and Privet Drive occasionally bizarre. This conflation of the real and the fantastical must of necessity deny the possibility of retreat from the perceived dangers of being a child in the twenty-first century, and ensure that children confront their demons as inevitably as they must recognise, in the portrayal of Hogwarts, the fact of their own control and surveillance in our contemporary world.

To return to the question of fidelity and the consensus view that *Harry Potter* the film is no match for *Harry Potter* the book, it could be argued that the film fails because it tries to be the book, or as close a copy as a film can be to a book, without realising what the consequences of such fidelity are. Filmic conventions, a prominent feature of the book, including postmodern intertextuality and cinematic devices, are strangely ignored in the film. While the film fails to copy a book, the book succeeds in copying a film and, in many ways, the books usurped the role of the film even before the film was released. The film disappointed viewers as it was a copy of the original which, as a copy, could not live up to the experience of the book, a book which is, effectively, more cinematic than its filmic adaptation and more comfortable with its status as fantastic narrative, which allows numerous symbolic outlets for contemporary childhood anxieties. Whether or not *Harry Potter and the Philosopher's Stone*, the book, has any merit as a 'film' or if it merely panders to a tired old Hollywood formula in order to achieve popular and commercial success, is another question to be asked. What is clear in the context of the 'fidelity' debate is that any film which prioritises transposition over interpretation is unlikely to recognise the pitfalls of aiming to bring the novel 'to life' and will, moreover, spectacularly fail by freezing all the action and events in an impossible simulacrum of the past made present.

6

Genre and Adaptation: Genre, Hollywood, Shakespeare, Austen

Due to the legacy left by Aristotle, we tend to take genre for granted. Aristotle, in the *Poetics*, describes genres, concentrating on comedy, tragedy and epic, and their features, as if they exist naturally rather than artificially – as if they can be plucked out of the air. Genre is often seen as something akin to a Platonic Form, something that has an ideal or divine status, what Hamlet describes as having 'a divinity that shapes our ends'. Northrop Frye, in the mid-twentieth century, following Coleridge, divides literary critics into *Iliad* critics and *Odyssey* critics[1] and attributes genre, as defined by the classical writers, with a mythic status; spring is associated with comedy, autumn with tragedy, winter with satire and summer with romance. Genre theory here is intimately connected to both the natural world and to Christian doctrine, that just as spring follows winter, individuals fall only in order to rise again.

The so-called rediscovery of the classical genres by Renaissance writers was not an unequivocal act of homage and imitation, as is evident from Shakespeare's attack on generic classification through Polonius's absurd list in *Hamlet*: 'tragedy, comedy, history, pastoral, pastorical-comical, historical-pastoral, tragical-historical, tragical-comical-historical-pastoral, scene individable or poem unlimited'.[2] Implicit in Shakespeare's critique of genre theory is the suggestion that genre is simply a tool used to obfuscate rather than clarify meaning. Certainly Shakespeare's plays, often themselves generic hybrids, all pose questions about their own individual genres. In addition to a central ontological problem with generic criticism is the word 'genre' itself. It has too many meanings: it reflects the compartmentalisation of literature into different structural types (epic, lyric, drama); it can relate to a work's relation with reality (fiction, non-fiction); it can be used to refer to sub-types within a broader genre (drama is broken into the genres of tragedy, comedy, romance) or it can reflect content rather than style or structure (the sentimental, romantic, historical, fantasy novel). The word 'generic' itself has come to mean what is common to all, often with derogatory connotations. While genre criticism is an approach that is fraught with problems, it is, nonetheless, common to both literature and film, especially Hollywood films which use generic classification for essentially commercial motives, as a means of packaging products, giving a clear indication to the consumer of what to expect. Just as cinema borrows its genres from literature, film produces additional genres – such as the western or the thriller – which feed back into literature.

Reading film criticism today, the literary origins of genre criticism are often forgotten or swept aside; for example, notwithstanding Homer, Virgil, Dante, Spenser or Milton, film-genre critic Steve Neale asserts that '"Epic" is essentially a 1950s and 1960s term.'[3] Such has been its dominance within Film Studies (as successor to auteurist approaches that regarded the director as the single creative force behind a film and hence the 'author'),[4] that 'genre theory' now seems to belong to the movies alone. Recognising its origins in literary genre criticism, Rick Altman establishes four basic paradigms for film genre: genre is used as (1) a blueprint, (2) a structure, (3) a label and (4) a contract.[5] The blueprint precedes the production, providing the film with a type of recipe; the structure is the proportion of the ingredients; the label is what the product says on the package; the contract is what the product promises the consumer. Genre is a way of soothing the audience, promising reaffirmation rather than something new, establishing expectations rather than challenging them. As mentioned previously, while seemingly sceptical himself about genre classifications, Shakespeare plays can be seen to be marketed according to 'genre', for instance it is *The Tragedy of Hamlet, Prince of Denmark, The Comedy of Errors* and *The Comical History of the Merchant of Venice*. Even literature on screen or adaptations – or more precisely 'the literary film' (which is more narrowly defined as canonical literature on film) – has been identified as a genre in itself, but one which, necessarily, borrows from other genres in order to capitalise on its cinematic rather than purely literary appeal.[6] The transformation of a literary text to screen is a change of one 'genre' to another and the demonstration of the imposition of film genres onto a literary text is one useful (but admittedly limited) way of explaining the process of adapting literature.

It would be Polonius-like to compile a complete list of film genres, especially as genre classification is becoming increasingly hybrid, less easy to pinpoint. Steve Neale has identified the following major film genres:

The Western
Comedy
Musical
War Movie
Thriller
Crime or gangster movie
Horror
Science Fiction
Detective
Epic
Social Problem Film
Teenpic
Biopic
Action-adventure

To this list, we add 'heritage', as a genre particularly relevant to literature on screen. Broadly speaking, 'heritage' films, like James Ivory's classic heritage film, *A Room with a View* (1986), aim to re-create a given period or text, giving an illusion of authenticity. However, recent debates in the subject have demonstrated the instability of any single definition of 'heritage', and, additionally, how the classification 'heritage' has gradually gathered negative connotations.[7] This is a problem that every genre classification faces. Diagnosing 'genre' has sometimes become a way of categorising or ranking movies, with genres coming in and out of favour, situated within an unofficial league table. While recognising that such taxonomic discourse (or labelling) is a critical construct, genre is a way of understanding and demonstrating both the aesthetic and economic factors underlying the reconstruction of a literary text to screen. In the early period of cinema, when film genres were newly emergent, movies were not identified, as they are today, in relation to a specific generic identity. For example, the Internet Movie Database now labels Orson Welles's *Othello* (1952), 'drama',[8] Tim Blake Nelson's *O* (2001), 'drama/romance/thriller',[9] William Dieterle and Max Reinhardt's *A Midsummer Night's Dream* (1935), comedy/fantasy/romance and Michael Hoffman's *A Midsummer Night's Dream* (1999), romance/fantasy.[10] Mindful of treading too far into Polonius-territory, identifying film genres does enable an understanding of why structural changes are made in translations from play to screen.

If we look at Steve Neale's list of major genres, it becomes apparent that Shakespeare's plays are remarkably malleable and have been translated into almost all of the major forms, each requiring different additions and deletions from the playtexts in order to conform to particular generic conventions. Recasting the plays into popular/contemporary formats or genres, like the teenpic, allows the genre itself a way of defending itself; as Douglas Lanier has argued, the presence of Shakespeare provides a popular genre with a way of defending itself, 'of suggesting its cultural importance, its worthiness of close study, its artistic value'.[11] The Japanese director, Akira Kurosawa, has been credited with turning Shakespeare's *King Lear* into a film which is as much recognisably Western as it Shakespearean. The wild landscape, peppered with the occasional horse, the ambivalence towards society, the insistence on masculine codes of behaviour and the prolonged silences and sparse dialogue in *Ran* (1985) are all evocative of the Western.

The introductory close-up of Tybalt's boots stamping out a cigarette and the shoot-out at the commencement of Baz Luhrmann's *William Shakespeare's Romeo + Juliet* (1996) also evoke Western conventions – but this is only one of numerous genres invoked in the first five minutes of the film, a succession of quick edits evokes the genres of gangster, police drama and the road movie. Drawing unmistakeable connections between what has become the iconic teen performance of James Dean in *Rebel Without a Cause* (1955) and Leonardo DiCaprio's Romeo, Shakespeare's play enters the genre of the teenpic in this 1996 adaptation. The youthfulness of the cast, the distinct social groupings including a 'brat pack' (consisting of the Capulet gang), the MTV use of contemporary popular music, the drunken house party, the comic/ineffectual father and the emphasis on Juliet's bedroom are all common features of the teenpic and equally prominent in other Shakespeare teenpics, such as Gil Junger's *Ten Things I Hate About You* (1998 – based on *The Taming of the Shrew*) and Tim Blake Nelson's *O* (2000 – based on *Othello*).

The vogue for different genres seems to come and go and Shakespeare auteurs, such as Kenneth Branagh, can be seen to capitalise on popular film trends. Made in the same period as *When Harry Met Sally* (1989), *Pretty Woman* (1990) and *Sleepless in Seattle* (1993), Branagh's *Much Ado About Nothing* (1993) is firmly situated within the romantic comedy genre. Branagh transforms Beatrice into a more independent woman who is allowed to speak through gestures at the end of the film. In the play, once Benedict asks for her hand in marriage, he literally 'stops her mouth' with a kiss, whereupon she becomes, like the typical Elizabethan dutiful wife, silent for the duration of the play. While Beatrice is empowered in Branagh's film, Benedict is softened, through the excision of his misogynistic remarks, especially the numerous cuckold jokes that litter the play. In his earlier *Henry V* (1988) Branagh turns to the genre of the war movie as a' way to transform the text for a late twentieth-century audience. The play's reported battle of Agincourt, as in Olivier's 1944 film, becomes the set piece of the film, and is shown at great length; but this time, unlike in the sanitised, 'beautiful war' scenes depicted by Olivier, the war is violent and muddy. Reminiscent of films about the Vietnam War (*Apocalypse Now*, 1979, *Platoon*, 1986 and *Good Morning Vietnam*, 1987), popular in the 1980s, Branagh gives us a view of war in all its horrors, but one in which there is the redeeming consolation of resultant comradeship. The film has been read within the context of both the war-film and buddy-film genre.[12]

Numerous examples of the 'film genrification' of Shakespeare could be cited. *Kiss Me Kate* (1953), *West Side Story* (1961) and *Love's Labour's Lost* (2000) are examples of Shakespeare: the musical. *Kiss Me Kate* changes the plot of *The Taming of the Shrew* by imposing another story onto the original play – it becomes a musical comedy in the vein of the 'let's put on a show' genre, a genre employed by a number of Shakespeare films, among them *Shakespeare in Love* (1998) and *Stage Beauty* (2005). Carrying his baggage as cannibal/murderer from *The Silence of the Lambs* (1991), Anthony Hopkins's presence alone transforms *Titus* (2000) into the film genre of horror. The plot of *The Tempest* overtly lends itself to the genre of science fiction and has been transformed into a prime example of the genre: *Forbidden Planet* (1956). One of the first Shakespeare films that could be classified a 'biopic', in which we are shown Shakespeare coming up with the idea for *Julius Caesar*, is Georges Méliès's *La Mort de Jules César* (1907), in which Shakespeare is played by the film director himself.

It's perhaps, not surprising that the biopic isn't a popular genre within the Shakespeare on Screen canon, with the notable and highly successful exception of *Shakespeare in Love*. Marc Norman and Tom Stoppard daringly adapt *Romeo and Juliet* and *Twelfth Night* into a film that oscillates between Shakespeare composing *Romeo and Juliet,* the rehearsals and performance of the play and the developing love story between the playwright and Viola De Lesseps (who becomes the prototype for Viola in the later comedy). Flaunting historical accuracy at almost every possible occasion, most notably ignoring the fact that Shakespeare adapted the play from an earlier work by Arthur Brook, perpetuating the Romantic notion that the true writer is inspired by what he experiences, the film mixes fiction with 'fact' to retell a fundamental biopic story of the journey to fame and the price that success brings.[13]

This genre, by its very nature, can be seen to operate as meta-adaptive, raising both the subject of adaptation – Shakespeare, we're told, like a modern scriptwriter, is 'only the author' – and the cost of success. Hollywood's penchant for genre is often regarded in relation to the industrialisation/conventionalisation of film, transforming narratives into a predictable repeatable, but successful formula. Hollywood has had an enormous role to play in the construction and perpetuation of film genre. As already mentioned, genre is used by Hollywood as a marketing tool and as a way of targeting a particular audience. Increasingly, Hollywood is producing complex generic hybrids, rather than single-genre films, undoubtedly with a view of increasing audience figures. Whinging writers aplenty over the last century have regarded scriptwriting as a mechanical, factory-driven exercise, one that embraces the conventional rather than the individual. Film genre is a part of the 'Hollywoodisation' or 'conventionalisation' of narratives, one of the unofficial conventions governing Hollywood production. Ken Gelder proposes that genre is one of the most productive ways of discussing popular fiction and that its generic visibility is what distinguishes it from canonical literature.[14] You could see genre film in the same light – just as readers of popular fiction actively look for examples of a particular genre, so too do film fans seek out particular types of film genres. However, it is important to distinguish the word 'genre' from 'generic'; narrative is not just conventionalised through genre, it is also reshaped according to a number of unofficial generic conventions. As Richard Maltby observes, Hollywood 'is a generic cinema, which is not quite the same as saying that it is a cinema of genres'.[15]

Genre/classic post-classic Hollywood and *A Midsummer Night's Dream*

Hollywood has been divided into two periods: 'Classic Hollywood' (from the mid-1920s to the late 1940s) and 'New Hollywood' (from the mid-1970s onwards). Whilst the latter has been seen to be 'post-generic', Neale argues that the division between the periods isn't as straightforward as it seems, that early twentieth-century cinema was not purely formulaic in terms of its adherence to a single genre, but full of examples of the generic hybrid.[16] Nonetheless, an awareness of film genres and Hollywood's generic conventions offers an insight into what happens when a play or novel is translated into a film.

Comparing William Dieterle and Max Reinhardt's 1935 *A Midsummer Night's Dream* with Michael Hoffman's 1999 version reveals different compositional rules relating to Classic and New Hollywood productions. The earlier film, observed to be the most ambitious adaptation of its time,[17] is at first remarkable for its painterly quality, the dramatic use of Mendelssohn's *Overture* to *A Midsummer Night's Dream* and his *Wedding March*, and its use of well-known actors from the Warner Brothers Studio, the 11-year-old Mickey Rooney, James Cagney, Dick Powell and Olivia de Havilland – in her first major part. Originally the film was criticised for taking too many liberties with the text, but compared to modern adaptations, it seems to retain much more than we would now expect. Reinhardt, an Austrian-born Jew, was living in exile in America at the time and it's tempting to read the film as a response to the growing threat of Nazism – surely the film uses black and white to reflect on two worlds, the forces of darkness and light, which would have a particular relevance for audiences of the mid-1930s. (Incidentally, the film was banned in Germany because its director was Jewish.) The German Expressionism of Reinhardt is perhaps at odds with the economic and cultural demands of Hollywood and Warners Studios, who produced the film.[18] 'The Triumph of Night' ballet is one of the most subversive and memorable sequences in the film and a visual articulation of the tension, central to the play, between the sexes, and where the women are unequivocally conquered. Set to Mendelssohn's mournful music, Oberon enters shrouded in a black cascading cape, accompanied by his black-clad entourage who individually abduct and carry away the bright female fairies whilst the set becomes increasingly dark, the music, incrementally oppressive. The sexuality of the scene is disturbing – the images suggest rape, violation, conquest and invasion. Titania is certainly made here to love a beast and the beast is clearly the menacing figure of Oberon, and not Bottom. This doesn't seem to belong to comedy, but does seem to draw out the more 'offensive' or darker dimensions of Shakespeare's text. There have been several versions of this film – its fantastic landscape is indeed filmic and it seems destined to be a part of the Dream Factory that is Hollywood. It's no accident that the next film to be discussed, released in 1999, begins with sprinklings of fairy lights, which we associate with the opening of Disney films and the figure of Tinker Bell: the fairy lights visually convey the message that 'the magic is about to begin'.

Directed by Michael Hoffman, this version, like Reinhardt's, draws on the appeal of famous stars such as Kevin Kline, Michelle Pfeiffer and Rupert Everett – and announces the influence of the earlier film by utilising the same Mendelssohn score. Looking at the surrender scene, however, the later film dilutes the violence; Oberon's unjust enforcement of Titania is almost forgotten, as Hoffman can be seen to be doing everything in his power to turn a complex and sometimes violent drama into a typical Hollywood romantic comedy. Clearly, literary narratives need to be reshaped in order to secure success on screen, and as Peter Quince prophetically reiterates, the production must not cause offence. Both versions of *A Midsummer Night's Dream* capitalise on the 'let's put on a show' genre. Both use the figure of Puck to direct the gaze – the early film's 11-year-old Mickey Rooney is disturbingly voyeuristic and mocking and the overall effect is one of menace and foreboding. He even follows Hippolyta and Theseus into their bedroom on their wedding night, at the close of the film. The older Puck of the 1999 version, played by Stanley Tucci, although mischievous, is somehow more reassuring and the closure is therefore more definite and satisfying.

In line with modern Hollywood films, Hoffman includes a number of 'quotation marks' to other films and modern preoccupations. The visit to the Fairy Bar at the beginning of the film, with its cast of fantastic characters, visually echoes the visit to the bar in the pioneering 1977 *Star Wars* in which Han Solo is introduced. The obligatory action sequence is provided in the sparring of Helena and Hermia; they turn into female mud-wrestlers, an ironic low cultural signifier in a seemingly high cultural film. The introduction of new technology offers Hoffman an opportunity to reflect on the subject of adaptation itself. Bottom's introduction of the gramophone to the fairies and Puck's discovery of the wonders of the bicycle are inserted as meta-adaptive moments, calling attention to the merging of the magic (or the dream) with technology, creating the Dream Factory that is Hollywood itself.

While both films extend the roles of the mechanicals, the latter film is Bottom-centred. Hoffman expands on Bottom's part, beginning and ending the film with Bottom, played by Kevin Kline. The unfunny practical joke in which his white suit is ruined by wine, at the beginning of the film, gives him a pathos and dignity, not in Shakespeare, and while Shakespeare's play unceremoniously disposes of the mechanicals in its closing moments, Hoffman concludes his film with the figure of Bottom, who takes Titania's fairy ring/crown in his hand, a visual confirmation (like Cinderella's shoe) that the magic is indeed real. As Judith Buchanan observes, while other productions have, in the bestialisation of Bottom, reaffirmed his position at the bottom of the social hierarchy, Hoffman's film elevates him, moving him from 'bottom' to top; his encounter with Titania transfigures and enriches him (both literally and metaphorically) for life.[19] Typical of Hollywood cinema, the film concludes with the central character moving from a lower to a higher social stratum, through the combined effects of love and sheer perseverance.

Identifying genres and generic conventions, while far from a science, provides a structure and vocabulary for placing and understanding the process of translation from literary text to film. As articulated here, the Hollywood genrification of literature is a 'dream factory', a semi-mechanical, commercially driven process that can be classified as a textual makeover, itself a generic convention, that takes a 'nerdy' text and makes it popular.

Jane Austen and genre

It's worth reminding ourselves (as stated at the beginning of this chapter) that genre begins with literature, that it's easy to see that writers like Shakespeare and Austen are instrumental to the development of film genre and that, with regard to genre, the relationship between film/television and literature is one of reciprocity. Today, critical attention to adaptations of Jane Austen's novels is second only to Shakespeare. But, as with Shakespeare, for most of the twentieth century such Austen adaptations were regarded as tawdry and unworthy of critical regard, mechanical and formulaic reconstructions of Jane Austen's work. Margaret Kennedy's lament in 1942 sums up attitudes to adaptations of Austen's work in the mid-twentieth century: Kennedy writes if Jane Austen were a screenplay writer, she would simply be asked to supply a story: '*Mr Collins proposes to Elizabeth* would have been thought sufficient.'[20] Kennedy's Romantic need for an 'author' blinds her to the merits of genre and mechanical reproduction. For her, 'film genre' and 'author' are totally incompatible.

But while Austen has been 'genrified' on television and film, her novels can be seen to provide a template for Hollywood genres, especially the romantic comedy. *Pride and Prejudice* (admittedly with its origins in earlier forms, including the likes of Shakespeare's *Much Ado About Nothing*) feeds the genres of 'screwball comedy' of the 1930s and 1940s as well as the romantic comedies of the late twentieth and early twenty-first centuries. As adapter Andrew Davies has stated, Austen is the easiest of all writers to adapt, partially because she is so precise in every detail but also because her work is arguably instrumental in establishing certain film and television genres.[21] The structure and basic plot of *Pride and Prejudice* can be seen to have had a direct influence on the Hollywood romantic comedy. (Although the initial plot is possibly borrowed from Shakespearean comedies, especially *Much Ado About Nothing* and *The Taming of the Shrew*.) Set at a time when culture is in flux, the book involves heterosexual couplings, misunderstandings and shifting perceptions. While challenging romantic clichés, it ultimately endorses them, with love triumphant in the end. Most importantly, the central couple commence the story as adversaries; their overt repulsion conceals to each other and themselves a covert attraction. *Pride and Prejudice* provides a formula for a specific type of romantic comedy: a couple vehemently arguing at the beginning of the film is normally a signal to the audience that they will end up married.

While there is an industry of Austen adaptations, especially after Andrew Davies's much heralded BBC adaptation of *Pride and Prejudice* in 1995, numerous other films could be classified as adaptations or, as Thomas Leitch has distinguished these very loose translations, 'allusions' of *Pride and Prejudice*:[22] to name just a few, *Bridget Jones's Diary* (2001), *When Harry Met Sally* (1989), *Pretty Woman* (1990) and Disney's *Beauty and the Beast* (1991). Each of these share a generic formula: a man and a woman disliking or dismissing each other for most of the film and becoming a couple at the end. The comedy results from misinterpretations of situations and characters. Equally influential on Hollywood cinema and television is *Emma* and the first story of a teen makeover. While *Clueless* (1995) self-consciously adapts Austen's text into a teenpic formula, numerous other films could claim kinship with Austen's *Emma* in their presentation of makeovers, cliques and self-deception. While 'genre films' have been condemned as form over content and genre over author (or *auteur*), ironically adaptations of *Austen* in the last decade of the twentieth and first decade of the twenty-first century have increasingly included an author or Austen figure in the narrative itself; if the valorisation of the author is 'anti-genre', ironically the imposition of the author's biography onto their stories is, ironically, another generic convention: the biopic. There seems to be no way of getting away from genre.

A recent example in this genre is *Becoming Jane* (2007), Austen's answer to *Shakespeare in Love*, implicitly announcing that Jane Austen adaptations are following in the footsteps of the now lucrative and ever-expanding Shakespeare-on-Screen domain. But the biographical reading of Austen's novels is hardly new. In both the 1980 and 1995 adaptations, it is Elizabeth who is given the famous first sentence – 'It is a truth universally acknowledged, that a single man in possession of a good fortune, must be in want of a wife' – establishing her as the 'authoritative' presence within the film. Later adaptations follow suit, such as Patricia Rozema's *Mansfield Park* (1999), where Fanny is the stand-in author, often shown recording her observations on the foul behaviour of her relatives and becoming at the end, with Edmund's help, a published writer. So too, ITV television adaptations of 2007 – *Mansfield Park*, *Northanger Abbey* and *Persuasion* – all invoke connections between author and heroine. Joe Wright's *Pride and Prejudice* goes so far as to introduce the film with Elizabeth entering the house, reading a book, a book that just happens to be *Pride and Prejudice* itself. The film begins with the covert message that Elizabeth is the author of her own story.

Steve Neale astutely observes that the biopic is, possibly, the most despised genre of all and accordingly, the genre has received little critical attention save for being the butt of the jokes of film critics, literary scholars and historians.[23] While we have reached a point in adaptation studies where it's now regarded as allowable, if not preferable, to transform a literary text, when it comes to a cinematic representation of an author, different rules seem to apply. In spite of the outrage of both the popular press and academics, the biopic's survival cannot be disputed. The Hollywood makeover of the author, while the last straw for some critics, has become a staple of recent years, with Joseph Fiennes as William Shakespeare, Kate Winslet/Judi Dench as Iris Murdoch, Gwyneth Paltrow as Sylvia Plath, Johnny Depp as J.M. Barrie, Renée Zellweger as Beatrix Potter, Philip Seymour Hoffman as Truman Capote, Nicole Kidman as Virginia Woolf and Anne Hathaway as Jane Austen.

Becoming Jane is an adaptation of *Pride and Prejudice* insofar as it magnifies parallels between Jane Austen's life and the novel, originally entitled *First Impressions*, begun in 1796, just prior to when the film is set. The film 'rewrites' Jane as both Lizzie (in her initial repugnance for the man she eventually loves) and Lydia (in her decision to run away with Tom). Typical of heritage adaptations, the film pays tribute to its own genre: the men stripping off and jumping into the lake references both *A Room with a View* and, of course, the 1995 BBC *Pride and Prejudice*. Jane's triumph at cricket echoes Greer Garson's Elizabeth's and Gwyneth Paltrow's Emma's victory at archery. The farm animals recall the 'rustic' scenes in the Joe Wright adaptation of *Pride and Prejudice* (2005), while there is a striking resemblance between Jane's cousin Eliza De Feuillide (played by Lucy Cohu) and Jennifer Ehle's Elizabeth of 1995. As well as an adaptation of Austen's novel, the film is also an adaptation of Jon Spence's biography of the author, *Becoming Jane Austen* (2003), in which Spence contends that *Pride and Prejudice* was inspired by the novelist's relationship with Tom Lefroy, the Irish nephew of Jane Austen's friend and neighbour – but while Jane is the reserved and proud Darcy figure, Lefroy, we are told, is more like Lizzie: he had five sisters to look after (and therefore couldn't afford an unconnected wife), his mother's maiden name was Gardiner, and, rather tenuously, the name 'Bennet' comes from Tom's favourite novel, *Tom Jones*.[24] For Spence, *Pride and Prejudice* is, on one level, a type of lovers' game, playfully littered with references to Tom and his family. Spence gives Jane Austen what she's successfully resisted for the last 200 years: a love life, indeed, he claims one so passionate that it inspired her to write and sustained her for life. According to Spence, 'Tom Lefroy did not dwindle into insignificance: he found his natural place in her imagination, and remained there for the rest of her life.'[25]

Biopics of authors are generally structured like a *Bildungsroman*, a portrait of the artist as a young person, concentrating on the events leading up to success and ending with the price that success brings. The emphasis is on the dawning of authorship, the 'becoming' the person we know as the author. The Romantic notion that art is inspired by love is also central to films depicting the life of an author. As Steve Neale explains, other common features include a conflict with a given community, prevalence of montage sequences, flashback sequences, trial scenes and/or a performance in public. *Becoming Jane* fits neatly into this template. But, somehow, once the recipe has been discovered, our taste for the product disappears.[26] This chapter has argued that the imposition of genre is a defining feature of popular literature and film and it is a feature that also decentralises the author. In essence, theoretically, the valorisation of the author and the imposition of genre cannot coexist. André Bazin's observation that adaptations can only be valued and analysed once we cast off what is, after all, a very modern and possibly flawed idea of the author, when applied to the biopic, raises a number of problems.[27] Paradoxically, the biopic – in particular the film biography of an author – uses genre both to kill and resurrect the author. But, on another level, the biopic – and this is certainly true of *Becoming Jane* – exemplifies Bazin's point about authority in that ultimately the author is shown to be purely a work of fiction.

7

A Simple Twist? The Genrification of Nineteenth-Century Fiction

As we discussed in the previous chapter, genrification of literary texts is both a way of revivifying and recontextualising a classic literary text for a new audience, sometimes in a new historical period or geographical location. Genre provides us with a way of talking about the translation from literary to film narrative, and in this chapter we would like to take this notion of 'genrification' further and explore three adaptations since the 1990s which have variously taken the work of George Eliot, Charles Dickens and Thomas Hardy, and produced genre films which 'make new' to varying degrees of critical and commercial success.

Whilst classic adaptation has long been an essential category in any book on adaptation worth its salt, those films that don't fit most available categories of the 'classic adaptation' and those which attempt a more populist genre-based response to the literary texts that they claim some relation to, are relatively neglected. The texts we will focus on in this discussion are all examples of this type of adaptation. *A Simple Twist of Fate* (MacKinnon, 1994), *Great Expectations* (Cuarón, 1998) and *The Claim* (Winterbottom, 2000) have an intertextual relationship to *Silas Marner* (Eliot, 1861), *Great Expectations* (Dickens, 1861) and *The Mayor of Casterbridge* (Hardy, 1886), respectively. All three adaptive texts share at least one feature in their narrative strategies, and that is to shift either historical or geographical location, or both, in order to 'update' the story itself (and in doing so, underline its 'timelessness') and/or to operate a critical rereading of the literary text which leaves us firmly with the indelible imprint of the director or, in one case, the lead star/scriptwriter. With such films, our first thought is not about visual resemblance to the idea of the historical period/ cultural space that the fictional text inhabits, and in all cases the script departs continuously from the language of the novels – even when thematic resonances remain. In their distinctive ways, all of these films encourage us to think further about the fate of texts which reject the prominent features of the classic adaptation and as such do not invite audience interest through the process of historical re-enactment. One of the reasons for looking at them here following our chapter on genre is that they all can be seen in their different ways to be asking us to think beyond the stranglehold of contemporary adaptation practices, which tend to adopt one mode of discourse to respond to classic adaptations and one mode to interrogate the popular. Moreover they gain little attention for being either 'classic' or 'popular'.

Common critical strategies in response to the classic adaptation all too often tend to operate within the confines of periodicity, costume drama and self-conscious reference to 'literariness', or to the author. Even after the bulge in well-received film and television adaptations over the past two decades, we think the use of the word 'confines' here is appropriate. We don't necessarily want to suggest that interesting and challenging things can't be done within these parameters – Sally Potter's *Orlando* (1992) and Patricia Rozema's *Mansfield Park* (1999) come to mind; yet the films we focus on here are flirting with well-known film genres (the Western, the romantic drama, the contemporary fairytale/parenthood movie), and in doing so remind us that each fertile period of nineteenth-century novel screen adaptations develops certain generic patterns which we only truly find remarkable when they are bent or challenged outright.

There are a number of key perspectives that we want to explore. The first issue which sets the scene is to rethink how canonical authors' presumed/invented identities and styles have pervaded and directed our expectations of an adaptation that is faithful in content or 'spirit'. Some of these screen authorial identities are so rigid that we can find their symbols peppered in popular culture – from the translation of Dickensian London to the 'Quality Street' sweet tin, to the crucial ballroom scenes in Austen adaptations sent up recently by UK comedians Armstrong and Miller;[1] what is apparent is that both TV and film adaptations exploit the same symbolic frameworks at any given time to such an extent that these symbols take on an iconic and directly meaningful significance. Different authors have different styles of costume and tone attached to them even down to soundtracks (compare again Austen and Dickens, Trollope and Eliot).

Additionally, the particular explosion of adaptations clustered around the mid-1990s, paralleled by a new dynamism in adaptation criticism, has established a template of critical approaches and possibly inscribed a model of the 'ideal-type' realisation of the nineteenth-century novel which means that such screen versions that have a relation to this 'template' tend to gain the most critical attention. We know also that the nineteenth century is somewhat unique in this: modernist novels have invited avant-garde or art-house responses; eighteenth-century adaptations are often playful, sexual or subversive in some other way, but it can't be denied that the nineteenth-century novel and its screen versions lie at the spine of adaptation studies, rivalled only by Shakespeare (but arguably the debates are discipline-specific here), with specialised sub-branches devoting themselves entirely to other single authors (Austen, Dickens, James, Hardy, the Brontës).

There is undoubtedly an insatiable hunger for the nineteenth-century adaptation from entertainment journalists and film and TV audiences alike: DVD and video technologies have meant that for two decades it has been possible to have numerous film versions from a number of periods at one's fingertips for comparison, or for sheer enjoyment. One side effect of the increasing availability and cheapness of back-catalogue films and TV series are that more are used overtly or covertly as aids to getting students to read texts they find difficult or out of kilter with their own experiences. The critical given – that over half of films released are adaptations of some form – does not detract from the core interest in the period of the nineteenth century and in the costume drama by extension. Whatever our disciplinary location we have come some way from the position articulated by Robert Stam, 'where film is perceived as the upstart enemy storming the ramparts of literature',[2] and inevitably producing dumbed-down, necessarily truncated 'versions' of literature. Recent years have seen numerous challenges to the prejudices that Stam is alluding to here, and more attention is given to the artistry of the films themselves, the generic location, the commercial and industrial context from which they emerge and the means by which audiences engage with them, negotiating pleasure beyond due reverence for a great author mediated on the screen.

It might be controversial to suggest that there is a critical 'template' we tend to apply to nineteenth-century adaptations which can close down areas of discussion, but there is some evidence for this, despite the probability that it has developed engaging perspectives and revisions of some of the most tenacious critical assumptions. At the least it prompts a focus on authorial identity, historical reimagining and the possibility of critical interventions or rereadings on the part of directors/screenwriters. It is only when we turn to texts whose intentions are quite different, possibly having a more tenuous relationship to critical rereadings, that we may be prompted to widen or change our response to classic adaptations, reflect back on dominant critical practices and rethink our critical strategies with regard to the nineteenth-century adaptation.

These 'genrified' adaptations bring different questions; they also give us pause to reflect, as Thomas Leitch does in a recent article, whether adaptation itself is a long neglected genre in film studies.[3] We also hope that by focusing on these examples, we can show what genrified adaptations tell us about adaptation in a commercial context – equally crucial in the production cycle of any film (or TV) adaptation. We have resisted the temptation to pass judgement on the 'success' of these films in aesthetic terms, beyond acknowledging their relative success in critical responses (or lack of them): inevitably when one comes to scrutinise texts for discussion it is often hard to remember whether you actually 'liked' them innocent of such a process. It may be that success could be measured by the ability or otherwise to travel over a number of audience communities, or for innovative readings of texts. We hope to ponder whether the chief function of these texts seems to reside in their presence as critical interpretations of the texts, the period, or chiefly the means by which they appropriate and remodel what are seen to be typically 'nineteenth-century' attitudes, beliefs and responses, for a latter period. As we have seen in the embracing of genrified adaptations of Austen such as *Clueless* (1995) and *Bride and Prejudice* (2004), shifting locations and ideologies can also yield new readings.

We once again pause to consider the fate of nineteenth-century-fiction on screen which crops up throughout this book and is the leitmotif of all critical writings of adaptation, as if the adaptations of nineteenth-century texts offer a kind of anchorage which guides us back to some essential precepts. However, when it comes to repurposing the nineteenth-century novel for other settings and other cultures, perhaps the rewritings in literary contexts, via the neo-Victorian novel, for example, are allowed more leeway, certainly in critical terms, than those on screen.

Alfonso Cuarón's 1998 adaptation of *Great Expectations* is a lavish updating of Pip's story, which is transplanted to Florida and New York City of the 1980s. Whilst the decision to update marks it out from the legion of other screen adaptations of this core text, it is worth remarking that this is one more 'New World' setting for a book that has been rewritten in literature in an Australian context more than once.[4] Lustig (Magwitch's character) in this film lacks any kind of postcolonial or oppositional political objective: rather, he represents destabilisation and chaos in his unspecified criminality, and signals the moment at which Finn's (Pip's) life is transformed. This is a romantic drama that strips away subplots and main plot tributaries to focus on the developing twisted relationship between Finn Bell and Estella (one of two characters in the film – Joe being the other – who retains the same name from the novel). The movie's tag line, 'let desire be your destiny', underlines this transfer to the genre of romance drama, announced symbolically as Estella's slapping of the young Pip in the novel transmutes into a precocious erotic kiss over a drinking fountain.

Magwitch (already demonstrating his capacity to rise from Dickens's novel like an autonomous folk hero in Peter Carey's *Jack Maggs*, published in 1997, the year before this film's release) has a significant, but mostly iconographic role; in another recent text, Dickens is reframed as cross-cultural literature of survival in Lloyd Jones's *Mr Pip* (2006 – set in Bougainville, once part of Papua New Guinea and now autonomous). As Brian McFarlane asserts in his recent book on the numerous adaptations of *Great Expectations,* despite the shifting focus on the romance narrative, in common with other film versions, this one feels the need to begin the film with the shock appearance of this criminal. Initially, Robert De Niro as Lustig seems to be reprising the sinister indestructible monster he played in the remake of *Cape Fear* (1991), or even of his lead role in Kenneth Branagh's *Frankenstein* (1994), but physically his shaven-headed appearance also recalls Finlay Currie's interpretation of the convict in David Lean's canonical 1946 film adaptation. Later, groomed and with plentiful hair to his shoulders, he pops up as amiable and cultured 'goodfella', with obvious Mafia associations meant to explain away his criminality without it having any further link to Finn's own story. Lustig's only remaining narrative function is purely as the means by which Finn can get a foothold in the New York art world (we never find out how Lustig makes his money); and he is murdered swiftly after their New York reunion.

The aspects of the novel dealing with the early scenes at Satis House are lovingly dwelt upon in this film, laying down the germs of what appears to be the narration of a thwarted love story told from Finn's perspective. Satis House becomes 'Paradiso Perduto', which in all its gothic finery recalls a different era of prosperity and social class divides, and is also reminiscent of the lavish film sets and costuming of classic Hollywood. During Finn's first visit to Paradiso Perduto, the images of love thwarted are brought to the fore, with the wreckage of a garden wedding feast abandoned and devastated by pests in the grounds of the house; set in opposition to this is his first view of Estella all in white, perhaps recalling the wedding gown of the novel's Miss Havisham. For the remainder of the film, both Ms Dinsmoor (the Miss Havisham figure, played by Anne Bancroft) and Estella wear shades of green, a personal motif of the director which, in this context, seems to connote jealousy (particularly Finn's, for their wealth and for Estella's suitors), nature (the house is being taken over by the environment slowly as if being swamped by nature), fertility, money and, perhaps, Finn's innocence. Dinsmoor is not a wreck in a wedding dress, but rather evokes a past redolent of cocktail parties and the idle rich, and is portrayed heavily made-up and in lavish cocktail outfits. She insists that Estella and Finn dance together, and their transition to young adulthood is achieved by a seamless dissolve from one scene to the next, where the older Finn and Estella (Gwyneth Paltrow and Ethan Hawke) continue to dance to the instructions of an unchanged Ms Dinsmoor.

Finn's vocation as artist adds a crucial dimension to the adaptation as a mode of dealing with the issue of first-person narration. Much has been written on the narrating voice in *Great Expectations* and such a textual example has been specifically militated in the study of adaptation (most notably by Brian McFarlane in his seminal *Novel to Film*), and the discussions about how (and if) one can capture narrative voice in film rage on. In Cuarón's film, Finn's art betrays the disjunction between his view of the world and a possible objective (third-person) retelling of his story. As the film opens, his charcoal drawings of fish are juxtaposed with a view of fish swimming in the water and accompanied by one of the many voiceovers in this film: 'I'm not going to tell the story the way it happened; I'm going to tell it the way I remember it.' His first portrait of the young Estella, executed on a piece of torn wallpaper among the detritus of Paradiso Perduto, physically blots out the 'real' Estella in front of him as the camera's point of view is located somewhere over his shoulder. Later Finn will draw her again in an extended scene where she comes to his apartment and poses unclothed (this is seen by her fiancé latterly as a means of speeding up their marriage) and we see her as Finn draws her – *film noir*-esque in fragments – focusing on the lips, eyes, breasts and crotch. Finn's first notebook is kept by Lustig after their watery encounter at the start of the film and comes to be the way in which Lustig promotes his expectations directed at his artistic talent – his trip to New York is specifically to allow him to work and exhibit. Lustig, Joe and Estella all feature so that these three characters represent the key influences on Finn's development as an artist.

It is Joe who becomes Finn's effective guardian (his sister leaves mysteriously when he is a child, having been shown entertaining lovers – or customers?). As in the novel, he is a benign, nurturant presence – a fisherman-cum-handyman eking out an existence on the Florida coast. Like the novel, one of the most affecting scenes featuring Joe is where he turns up unexpectedly – in this case, at Finn's gallery opening in New York. His clumsy and enthusiastic gaucheness is juxtaposed with Finn's constipated attempts to act the successful artist (one aspect of which was having created a fiction about Joe's early death as a drug smuggler in order to mythologise himself further as the lone artist). This scene is rapidly followed by the visit of Lustig to Finn's apartment and the revelation that he is the source of Finn's wealth, only rapidly to end in tragedy, as in true gangster fashion he is pursued and gunned down in front of Finn on the subway. This moment of tragedy only impels Finn's return to Joe (now with new partner and child) in Florida and a reunion with Estella at Paradiso Perduto, with her young daughter acting as a visual prompt of the younger Estella: the daughter wears a more cheerful shade of peppermint green and Finn and Estella mirror each other in white, as if cleansed of the shade of Ms Dinsmoor and their past.

The key focus of the film is on the relationship between Finn and Estella and we have left significant discussion of this to last for that reason. The novel's Estella is conveyed as pure, cold and desexualised; in Cuarón's adaptation, pronounced a 'genuinely sexy take on that tale of romantic obsession' by Brian McFarlane,[5] Estella is comfortable with her own desires. She precociously French-kisses Finn while still pre-pubescent and later, after having Finn rescue her from a dull cocktail party, she goes to his house and lets Finn masturbate her in a room surrounded by her portraits, only to leave promptly once satiated. The film encourages us to perceive a disjunction between Estella's mobilisation of sexual desire and Finn's idealisation of her through his paintings, emphasising the partiality of this first-person narrative account, and also offering us what has become an almost compulsory neo-feminist revision of the nineteenth-century heroine. The scenes which foreground their attraction are celebratory and romantic, and the detail of her relationship with her fiancé remains largely in the background.

Her life among the wealthy, feckless socialites of Manhattan, not being Finn's concern, is not ours in a film that requires Finn's presence in lieu of first-person point of view. Michael J. Johnson's sense that 'Cuarón's film is neither Dickens's novel nor Lean's movie – but … is clearly aware of and playfully allusive to both the novel and the earlier film'[6] is self-evidently true in one respect (not least in the choice to retain the novel's title and therefore that of Lean's film). By making such comparisons, however, it would be far too easy to underestimate what is most striking about this film, which is the way it exposes the fallaciousness and yet the tenacity of Finn's fantasies of Estella's sexual and social power; Finn's earlier assertion that he tells the story as he remembers it rather than as it happened allows us to view the final romantic reunion of a white-clad Estella and Finn (as purified of social contamination) with some scepticism.

Arguably unlike *Great Expectations, Silas Marner* is not an obvious choice for modernisation; one notes from the outset that from the point of view of an adapter looking for periods of intensity of action, this is a strangely unbalanced book – in that over half of it precedes the appearance of Eppie at Silas's cottage, focusing instead on the changing fates of both Silas and Godfrey Cass – Silas the innocently wronged and Godfrey the guilty. Key themes are assiduously positioned in order to form the discursive backdrop to the events which follow, including the mixture of blind religiosity and superstition which governs the evangelical church community and which exiles Silas from its midst. The discoveries of who stole Silas's money and who is Eppie's natural father are concentrated towards a conclusion which offers few of the reconciliations that are required when Hollywood takes up such a story. Godfrey Cass does not succeed in making his claim upon the child; Silas does not find answers or clear his name in his attempted return to Lantern Yard (which has been obliterated by a huge factory), but rather finds the past has been erased. Fate and just desserts vie for position here and like Elizabeth-Jane for Henchard in *The Mayor of Casterbridge* in different circumstances, Eppie becomes the most precious gift for Silas.

Q.D. Leavis notes the influence of Christian in *Pilgrim's Progress* on Silas; she also acknowledges its importance to Thomas Hardy, and looking at Michael Winterbottom's *Mayor of Casterbridge* and Gillies Mackinnon's *A Simple Twist of Fate* in tandem, there are some thematic overlaps, especially in the deployment of fate and spiritual reward. Fate and guilt lie at the heart of the *Mayor of Casterbridge* too; Henchard has to live silently with the guilt of selling his wife, and in recompense gives up drink for 21 years. The country people in both novels are seen as equally chary of strangers and embracing of a fatalistic view of fortune. In *The Mayor of Casterbridge*, Henchard represents a bygone era and old ways, achieving wealth and dominance through a kind of patriarchal dominance; whereas Farfrae will bring in the new and with it a new manifestation of democratising masculinity. Farfrae appeals to the sentiment of the community and rules through fairness, dignity and courtesy – his instinct for the right gesture and response endears him to a people used to be dealt with roughly (though kindly in some cases, if we think of the example of Henchard's paternalistic care of Whittle's mother, remembered by Whittle when he sees Henchard and helps him in his last days). Susan is depicted as gullible, pious and limited, Elizabeth Jane as questing for self-improvement and capable of great love and forgiveness, and who reconciles herself to Henchard, even though her attempts are too late. The narrator's closing paragraph of the novel indicates Elizabeth Jane's growth as a character and the stark lessons she learns about life: 'in being forced to class herself among the fortunate she did not cease to wonder at the persistence of the unforeseen, when the one to whom such unbroken tranquillity had been accorded to the adult stage was she who youth had seemed to teach that happiness was but the occasional episode in a general drama of pain'.[7]

Besides the betrayal of his wife and daughter, Henchard's other 'crime' is perhaps his complicity in the damaged reputation of Lucetta, after their love affair when she nursed him back to health in Jersey. Naturally it is Lucetta who pays the highest price for that shame: after the skimmington ride she dies and loses her unborn child. It is as if both dishonoured women – Susan and Lucetta – have to be dispatched before Elizabeth Jane can grasp at fulfilment (temporary though it may be) in her future with Farfrae. For all his modern methods in business, Farfrae is unreconstructed when it comes to women. His transition from Lucetta to Elizabeth Jane is smooth as if Lucetta's only function was to show that Farfrae could literally take everything from Henchard – and perhaps to show a similarity in their marked physical needs, so strongly repressed by Henchard.

Winterbottom's revisionist Western takes on Hardy's portrayal of Henchard as both physically domineering and sexually voracious, showing him punishing a petty thief by personally whipping him, by being ready to challenge all comers with his gun and by his energetic sex life with his lover Lucia, later juxtaposed by a much more tender and asexual bedroom scene with his wife Elena. *The Claim*,

set in the Sierra Nevada mountains in California of 1867, has Henchard
as Daniel Dillon (played by Peter Mullan), the pioneer prospector,
selling his wife for a bag of gold and the claim that goes with it, and
literally carving the town of Kingdom Come out of the mountains. Just
as Casterbridge is described as having no border from the agricultural
environment around it, as 'county and town met at a mathematical
line',[8] so Kingdom Come is dwarfed by the mountains and its lines
blurred by the persistent snow. The original cabin of Burns (the man
to whom he sells his wife and daughter) is almost obscured by nature;
and in a flashback to Dillon remembering his first arrival to this cabin
with wife and child, Dillon, enveloped in a blizzard, is barely distin-
guishable as a person; similarly Dalglish (the Farfrae character) and
his men are dwarfed by their environment as they try to carve a way
through the mountains to build the railway.

The Claim strips the story down and simplifies the motivations of
Henchard: here fate and its vicissitudes are represented by the huge-
ness of the snowy landscape which dwarfs its inhabitants, and pioneer
life is presented with some Western staples – the clapboard buildings,
women as prostitutes, and bar scenes with sexually frustrated prospec-
tors. Winterbottom offers few nods to coherence and the flashbacks
showing the drunken Dillon's swapping of wife and child for a bag of
gold are confusing at first. Similarly in the scene where Dillon arranges
for his house to be moved, in its entirety, down the hill, it is not always
clear what the time sequence is; but, as has been noted by Gayla S.
McGlamery, the visual homage to German new-wave film makers
such as Rainer Werner Fassbinder, Werner Herzog and Wim Wenders,
as well as the Japanese director Akira Kurosawa,[9] is clear.

Winterbottom is no stranger to Hardy, having adapted *Jude the
Obscure* in 1996, though at that time he opted for similar period and
location, transferring Christminster to Edinburgh. As with Cuarón's
Great Expectations, The Claim is cinematographically stunning and the
environment conveys emotions, so that the sometimes frustrating psychological *volte-face* of characters in the *Mayor* can be skimmed over,
it being understood that their emotions, are symbolically rather than
realistically drawn. Natassia Kinski's role as Elena, the mother in this
film, also gestures back to her role as Tess in Polanski's film adaptation
of that Hardy novel; yet her virtually mute performance emphasises
the slight grasp these individuals have over their own survival and
their initial dependence on the ubiquitous Dillon, who has literally
created this town which is precariously established within the unin-
habitable surroundings that always threaten to engulf it. Henchard's

fatal self-destructiveness is translated into Dillon's destruction of his town (which for the reasons mentioned above is essentially a reflection of him). The old order of the pioneers following the gold is usurped by the new order of the demands of the railway and its promise of riches; Dalglish's decision to pass by Kingdom Come threatens its very existence and Dillon gives himself up finally to the hostile environment as the town is consumed by fire.

The Western in its 'classic' form, as has been noted many times, fell out of favour in the latter half of the twentieth century because of its portrayal of unreconstructed masculinity, imperialism and sexism: but here Winterbottom, in common with *Last of the Mohicans* (Michael Mann, 1992), and perhaps anticipating another even more successful Western adaptation, *Brokeback Mountain* (Lee 2005), revivifies the genre and gives it an art-film inflection. In common with Cuarón's vision for *Great Expectations*, Winterbottom's adaptation of *The Mayor of Casterbridge* is a fiercely independent adaptation which at the same time embeds an understanding of previous classic adaptations in its intertextual wake. Via his claim, Dillon enacts one man's futile attempts to gain mastery over nature (and women) in his building of Kingdom Come and his buying and selling of women (he pays Lucia off with the deeds of the Saloon once he decides to end the relationship); after the town is destroyed the film finishes with an aerial shot of men 'prospecting' for bars of gold in the ruins of the bank. *The Claim* might also be seen as an interim stage in Winterbottom's own intervention in the field of adaptation studies as he moves from *Jude* to *The Claim* to the seemingly unfilmable in *A Cock and Bull Story* (2005); interestingly in this case the further he moves away from fidelity or the eighteenth- and nineteenth-century 'template' of the period-specific costume drama, the more he moves towards commercial and critical success.

MacKinnon's *A Simple Twist of Fate*, scripted by and starring Steve Martin, becomes a film keen to draw out the fairy-tale elements of the novel into the feel-good fable, as well as keying into other contemporary film 'cycles', most notably the 'fatherhood' films, as discussed in Chapter 4, including *Three Men and a Baby* (1987), *Parenthood* (1989, starring Martin), *Hook* (1991), *Mrs Doubtfire* (1993) and *Cheaper By the Dozen* (2003 – also starring Martin). The core theme of this film is the redemption offered by children, but Michael McCann's (Martin's) good fortune after the denial of natural fatherhood when his wife reveals that her unborn child has actually been fathered by his close friend is juxtaposed with John Newland's (Gabriel Byrne's) misfortunes: having refused to acknowledge the child of his drug-addict girlfriend as his, he is punished with a wife who miscarries and with a daughter who chooses to remain with her adoptive father.

McCann, like Silas, locks himself away from humanity after the betrayal by his wife and friend. His miserliness and love of gold (the most anachronistic feature of this modern take on *Silas* if one were trying to read it as a realist film) is ironically triggered by his false friend's gift of a gold coin as an investment for what he believes to be his unborn child. Some years later and after one too many celebratory drinks, McCann becomes reckless with his gold whilst admiring his growing collection, allowing for Newland's amoral brother Tanny to steal the coins after crashing his brother's car and killing the passenger, Mathilda's natural mother. The mother, Marsha Swanson, is portrayed as deeply protective of her child but fatally flawed because of her heroin addiction, just as Molly in *Silas* has succumbed to the 'Demon Opium'.[10] Newland's political ambitions, combined with his desire for the socially acceptable Nancy, determine his fate in this morally two-dimensional fable; McCann, like Silas, feels that Mathilda has replaced his stolen gold and she later chooses her natural mother and him as her 'real' parents. As in all good parenthood movies, McCann has to 'learn' the skills the hard way, tutored by single mother April Simon and her son Lawrence – straight replacements of Dolly Winthrop and her son Aaron in *Silas Marner*. McCann's methods are eccentric and anachronistic as he pushes her around in an antique pram, and his method of tethering Mathilda and trying (and failing) to punish her is imported straight from the novel (and held against him later in the courtroom). Critics slated the film, unlike Martin's 1987 scripted adaptation *Roxanne*, which was a box-office success. There he was on the sure ground of romantic comedy, a genre in which he had a good track record; here the lack of comedy defied people's expectations of a Martin film vehicle: as *The Washington Post* lamented, 'As a comic, Martin soars, but here he has clipped his own wings.'[11] In some ways, of the three examples discussed in this chapter, *A Simple Twist of Fate*, although an updated version, attempts the closest 'fidelity' to plot in the way it retains elements which are historically anachronistic – so that at times there are moments when Martin seems to unthinkingly attempt to translate a scene from *Marner* and revel in its 'olde worlde' anachronisms. This empty celebration of 'pastness' – the collecting of gold coins, the vintage toys and prams, the timelessness of the small-town setting – is another dimension to the classic adaptation which refuses the 'classic' template and will be evident (though more sophisticated) in the example of *Cruel Intentions* in the following chapter. At other times the film becomes a mess of genres, as in the courtroom drama it briefly (and pointlessly) descends into during the latter stages of the film. Earlier, the baseball scene could be straight out of *Parenthood* or *Hook,* and the discovery of the skeleton of Tanny Newland in the quarry takes us back to realms of the gothic or fairy tale.

Of the three films discussed *A Simple Twist of Fate* aims for the highest degree of interpretive excess and its visual codings clash confusingly. While the other two films may confuse or frustrate (the dialogue in *The Claim*, the strangeness of the 'romance' in *Great* Expectations, for example), visually they offer a coherent generic set of codes which both allow for an identification with films and other commercial productions in like genres or cycles, while focusing on selected aspects of the novels, in a positioning that is strictly anti-classic adaptation.

These three films provide much material for analysis of adaptations which are not of a genre but which 'genrify' their hypotext, if we may be allowed such a clumsy construction; not commercial blockbusters but nonetheless produced with an eye to the popular market, they exploit core film genres and audience groupings. Winterbottom has 'form' as a serious and challenging director and his Western makes few concessions to the single-time viewer; his habit of encouraging actor improvisation equates with the notorious taciturnity of the average Western hero and is at times effective in capturing such a generic association. At the same time, masculinity is held under scrutiny by the juxtaposition of Dillon and Dalglish; yet Winterbottom's engagement with the sexual as in itself radical (his *9 songs*, 2004, was controversial for its 'real' sex scenes) possibly prevents an equally searching interrogation of femininity in *The Claim*. Cuarón also has the credibility to be taken seriously as an arty/commercial director (his 2004 *Prisoner of Azkaban* released Harry Potter from the 'children's film foundation' woodenness of the first two adaptations, as we discussed in Chapter 5). But Martin, who although not the director, is most associated with *A Simple Twist*, is poleaxed first by the audience expectations of an accomplished comic performance and by the generic incoherence of the film itself, reaffirming the importance of generic identifications to anchor an audience and its interpretation of what it sees on screen.

Successful or not, all these films exemplify the fate of the classic novel in the era of cross-media fertilisation; the lack of instant recognition as adaptations (except for *Great Expectations* which, as the only film in this selection to retain the novel's title, announces its relation to both Dickens's work and numerous other screen adaptations) may in some cases be compensated for by fan communities who share their pleasures of unravelling texts online. Such intertextual engagements with nineteenth-century fiction place a greater premium on reinvention through refunctioning and reimagining and force us to think beyond the givens of heritage or costume drama.

We would assert that these three texts are at one and the same time comfortably compatible with the mid-1990s explosion of the 'new' sexy costume drama, pushing for their own commercial success by deploying familiar genre tropes in new ways. Adaptations that increasingly extend parameters and safe 'templates' of adapting are in part also a result of changing responses to adaptation and its cultural value, both within the industry and also within the academic environment, and are a necessary product of a discourse of adaptation in commercial reviews which encourage readerly sophistication and active enjoyment of the suspension of the simple pleasures of the costume drama by the active exposure of the process of adaptation itself – as in *Adaptation* (2002) or *A Cock and Bull Story* (2005).

Robert Stam has noted that '[m]any revisionist adaptations of Victorian novels meanwhile, "de-repress them" in sexual and political terms; a feminist and sexual liberationist dynamic releases the sublimated libidinousness and the latent feminist spirit of the novels and of the characters, or even of the author, in a kind of anachronistic therapy or adaptational rescue operation.'[12] The most successful adaptations of nineteenth-century novels have offered such 'relief' or purgative remedies in rejecting obsolete ideologies in favour of positing 'challenging' new ones that are actually highly compatible with contemporary high liberal world views. Christine Geraghty's view is that our attachment to nineteenth century sources isn't necessarily about our intimate knowledge of the source but 'rather on the story being available through a range of other sources including children's abridged versions, plays, comics, radio, and musicals, as well as film and television',[13] and that the act of comparing 'versions' through DVD collections and TV reruns is part of the pleasure of experiencing classic literature. For this reason, Geraghty would argue, numerous adaptations 'can close down, rather than open up, interpretative possibilities'.[14] These adaptations may in part offer a challenge to Geraghty's position here, although she might see them as rarities as 'they pull away too much from the connections to previous versions and lose the cultural values associated with a classic adaptation'.[15] Arguably they are seeking to gain the kind of audience cachet associated with innovative genre restyling, and in Cuarón's *Great Expectations* we perhaps see a homage to Whit Stillman's *Metropolitan* (1990) which, as a loose response to *Mansfield Park* and also in its New York moments, focuses on a hedonist group of young rich kids in the 1980s who could almost feature in a classic Hollywood film of the 1930s or 1940s. Tom, the only middle-class man amongst this group of super-rich debutantes and their beaux, confirms Geraghty's view about the multiple ways we gain access to the 'source', in that his views on Austen are derived entirely through Lionel Trilling, reinforcing the film's own 'distance' from *Mansfield Park* by costume drama standards and its continuation of the critical debate about the likeableness or otherwise of Fanny Price, amongst other things.

Looking at these films through the lens of genre reminds us, as Neale points out, that 'Genres do not consist solely of films. They consist also of specific systems of expectation and hypothesis which spectators bring with them to the cinema and which interact with films themselves during the course of the viewing process.'[16] In re-enacting some forms of genre, such as Winterbottom's summoning of the Western, it is not only the 'source' text which is being refunctioned but that generic space itself, even if it also offers a seamless homage to the Western of yesteryear which is about 'men's fear of losing their hegemony and hence their identity, both of which the Western tirelessly reinvents'.[17] For Stam, 'adaptations redistribute energies and intensities, provoke flows and displacements; the linguistic energy of literary writing turns into the audio-visual-kinetic-performative energy of the adaptation, in an amorous exchange of textual fluids.'[18] This rather messy and visceral exchange envisaged by Stam also reminds us that in performing genre, adaptation itself is in some senses a genre – particularly if we agree with Leitch that 'If there is indeed a Henry James genre, a Jane Austen genre, a classic-novel genre, and a heritage genre, it requires on a short step to postulate the even more capacious genre of adaptation itself.'[19] We are not sure, and neither perhaps is Leitch, that the assertion of a genre of adaptation helps us in the evaluation of its multiple and diverse products, but in the use of genre to imagine our relationship to the text we immediately summon the existing ur-text, the economics, the cultural artefact and the audience as part of the adaptation process in a trans-literate environment that has fewer and fewer needs for the re-enactment of pastness.

8

Les Liaisons Dangereuses:
Letters on Screen

There has been some discussion in recent years about 'unfilmable' books, and also the film industry itself has engaged with such phenomena – as has already been noted, examples are *Adaptation* and *A Cock and Bull Story,* celebrated as cultishly unreadable. There are also films about the failure to adapt – for instance Keith Fulton and Louis Pepe's *Lost in La Mancha* (2002). Choderlos de Laclos's *Les Liaisons Dangereuses* (1782) might seem on the face of it to present similar problems to those posed by Laurence Sterne's *Life and Opinions of Tristram Shandy* (1759), its epistolary framework presenting some challenges to the film adapter, not least that a defining event in the novel – the death of Valmont – cannot be directly narrated. After letter 162, which comprises Danceny's challenging of Valmont to a duel, the final 12 letters follow rapidly, and anti-climatically wrap up the drama with the death of Madame de Tourvel, the flight of Danceny and news of the hideous disfigurement and escape of the Marquise de Merteuil.

Unlike Sterne's shaggy-dog story, which is itself an account of the failure to adapt a 'life' into art, *Les Liaisons Dangereuses* has a narrative which impels it forward. The epistolary form is used to superb effect in this novel (Laclos's debts to both Richardson's *Clarissa* and Rousseau's *La Nouvelle Héloïse* are inscribed intertextually). Characterisation, location, intense periods of drama are all narrated in the second degree, sometimes with vying perspectives on the same event (for example, the 'rape' of Cécile Volanges). The letters are crucial to connect threads of a plot enacted in different locations, and the key letter writers (Valmont and Merteuil) mire the reader helplessly in a plot which gathers momentum as well as victims, as innocence is devalued, and love is overlaid by strategies of seduction couched in terms of military conquest. Of course the pleasures of reading *Les Liaisons Dangereuses* are bound up by the sensation of ourselves being in the thrall of these two characters and the fact that, as Merteuil reminds us, 'there is no one without a secret which it is in his interest never to reveal'.[1]

Epistolary novels, like diary novels, have as a large part of their appeal the positioning of the reader as voyeur; for what is more deliciously taboo than reading someone else's letters or diaries? Of course there is also a convention in literature that someone who reads someone else's private papers is not to be trusted and will also have to carry the burden of knowledge of something not meant for their eyes which, if revealed, could compromise everyone around them. The exchange of letters in *Les Liaisons Dangereuses* reinforces this old adage and in this context underlines a key theme of the novel – that of the ways in which society represents a code of behaviours and moral certainties which are recklessly disregarded by all of its members. As the novel progresses it seems that few are exempt from corruption. The letters as *letters* are crucial in many ways to our understanding of the novel's themes, in that they represent a social subtext where the utterance of taboos and the confession of sins and desires expose the frailty of society's code of behaviours, more so as the two protagonists operate within society, rather than from its margins.

An epistolary novel demands certain key structural principles for the narrative to evolve. First someone has to 'compile' the letters in the form in which we receive them and provide a justification for their collection – in this case, the means by which all these letters might be bundled together is largely organic to the novel's climax. Valmont passes on his own collection to Danceny after their duel and Danceny has already had access to some through Merteuil's selective revelations, with which she sought to finally triumph over Valmont. Those others, such as Cécile's to her schoolfriend or Madame Rosemonde's correspondence with Monsieur Bertrand at the end, are not so easy to account for by the circulation of the letters as revealed in the novel itself, hence the significance of the Editor's Preface, which at once confirms the provenance of these letters and at the same time allows a respectable distance for the Editor from the content of them. While the Editor uses the veracity of the letters to distance himself from any immoral intentions, the Publisher's Note casts doubt on their authenticity or at least on their status as contemporary documents, asserting: 'we never see young girls today with an income of sixty thousand *livres* taking the veil, nor any Présidente who is young and pretty dying of a broken heart'.[2] The stated purpose of the publication of the letters, according to the Editor, is because 'it is doing a service to society to unveil the strategies used by the immoral to corrupt the moral'.[3] Both these narrative framing functions only serve to whet the implied reader's appetite and also provide a moral justification for their publication, so that salacious detail can be savoured under the pretence of a wider public good.

An epistolary novel places particular demands upon its readers in that all events are told in the past tense and are mediated through the narrative of the letters; multiple correspondents imply multiple perspectives, but quickly in this case we come to realise that we have two main narrators – Valmont and Merteuil – who, to a large extent, control events and their interpretation. They are both libertines, but through the novel it is reinforced to us that male and female libertines (the latter almost an oxymoron by eighteenth-century models of female behaviour) have to act differently. Valmont is a known rake and yet his social standing makes him tolerated in all areas of society; Merteuil is from the outside a respectable widow with an unimpeachable reputation, and part of her skill is in demonstrating how successfully she maintains this illusion of her respectability, even as her exploits implicate her more deeply. Valmont is seen to enjoy the fact that his social status exempts him from answering to others about his moral choices and impels him to take further and further risks until the final duel is seen as an inevitable consequence.

Early letters pit the naivety and romantic longings of Cécile against the machinations of the libertines, and before long the reader finds it impossible to read any of the letters except through the lens of Valmont's and Merteuil's interlocking plots for revenge. As the narrative progresses this practice becomes necessary to understanding the progress of events, as Valmont, anxious to know who is muddying his name to the object of his desire, Madame Présidente de Tourvel, intercepts her post and discovers the culprit to be Madame de Volanges, which encourages him to accept Merteuil's challenge to deflower Madame de Volanges's daughter Cécile (although Merteuil's motives for revenge satisfied by the defloration of Cécile are directed against her ex-lover Gercourt). The circulation of letters becomes more complex as Valmont forwards some on to Merteuil, including copies of his own love letters to Madame de Tourvel, so that she can vicariously enjoy his seduction upon which their wager is based. Later letters will be selectively revealed to provide partial and distorting truths – as in the case of Merteuil's seeming revelations to Danceny, which prompts his duel with Valmont.

In an intriguing conclusion to the novel our contact with the two key protagonists is suddenly cut off and we are left to read of Valmont's death in a letter from Monsieur Bertrand to Madame Rosemonde and, via Madame de Volanges, the fates of Merteuil, de Tourvel and Cécile. Without the interpretive commentaries of Valmont and Merteuil how are we, pushed back into the realm of social proprieties, to assimilate this? This ending exposes the frustrations as well as the potentialities of the epistolary form; we have to determine ourselves whether Valmont's death is a deliberate act of self-destruction, whether he did actually love either de Tourvel or Merteuil and, similarly, whether Merteuil's despair is prompted by love of Valmont. Her disfiguring illness and social disgrace provide ample punishment for her crimes and offer the kind of closure demanded by censors: unfortunately the sequel detailing the continued adventures of Merteuil (and Cécile) hinted at in the conclusion is never realised.

In what remains of this chapter we focus on five film adaptations of *Les Liaisons Dangereuses*, all produced since 1959[4] – they are *Les Liaisons Dangereuses* (Roger Vadim, 1959), *Dangerous Liaisons* (Stephen Frears, 1988), *Valmont* (Milos Forman, 1989), *Cruel Intentions* (Roger Kumble, 1999) and *Untold Scandal* (Je-yong Lee, 2003) . Two of these adaptations retain the geographical and historical location of Laclos's novel; two move the action to their contemporary period, one set in France and one in the United States (New York), and *Untold Scandal* maintains an eighteenth-century setting but moves it to Korea. *Dangerous Liaisons*, Christopher Hampton's adaptation of his own successful stage version of the novel, commands a kind of critical centrality as the defining adaptation (as impossible to escape as David Lean's *Great Expectations*), as revealed by the homage paid to it by both *Cruel Intentions* and *Untold Scandal*. It must also be noted that Milos Forman's *Valmont*, its release delayed to allow an interval of time after the release of *Dangerous Liaisons*, is very much the victim of the latter's triple Oscar-winning success. Although in some ways *Valmont* offers one of the more innovative retellings, the impact of the relatively low budget ($15 million to *Valmont*'s $35 million[5]) of *Dangerous Liaisons* obscured its virtues for most contemporary viewers.

Roger Vadim's *Les Liaisons Dangereuses* is at once a homage to a novel which travelled generically from notoriously immoral bestseller (Marie Antoinette was said to have possessed a copy which she had

bound without the title or author's name on the cover) to a French literary classic, and a reframing of that narrative by transplanting it into
contemporary French cultural mores of the bourgeoisie. Also known
as *Les Liaisons Dangereuses 1960,* this title suggests that the film looks
to the future rather than to the past, and that its characters are challenging existing moral certainties by testing them against their own
'moral' compass. Shot in black and white, *Les Liaisons Dangereuses*
emerges at the time of the *nouvelle vague,* and Vadim has clear artistic
links with and is a contemporary of Truffaut, Godard and Rohmer,
even though literary adaptations were not a dominant feature of the
movement. Jeanne Moreau, who played Juliette (Merteuil), is a key
new-wave actor and would go on to star in *Jules et Jim* (1962) years later,
and become an emblem of modern female sexual self-determination.
Valmont (played by Gérard Philippe) is said to be modelled on Vadim
himself as depicted in his autobiography *Memoirs of the Devil* (1975),
and in an interview Vadim asserted, echoing Gustave Flaubert perhaps, 'Valmont? C'est moi!'[6] If Valmont can be seen to represent
the sexual excesses of the latter part of the twentieth century this is
emphasised by the intriguing move of marrying him to the Merteuil
figure, Juliette. Whereas in the novel these characters' machinations
were a dark subcultural activity in which moral order can be restored
to society's surface, this modern 'open' marriage mounts a more direct
challenge to the most central of social institutions, and allows Valmont
and Juliette to be portrayed as more directly supporting each others'
quest for pleasure beyond a marriage that has protected itself again
ennui by such means. The society represented by the establishing scene
in the film emphasises the indolent decadence of the French haute
bourgeoisie, and the background visuals to the credits, which focus
on a chessboard, emphasise that Juliette and Valmont's machinations
have in the past been diversions rather than romances – a chess game.
Valmont, the rake, becomes Valmont the playboy in Vadim's film, and
in order to emphasise his idle malignity:

> Vailland and Vadim settled upon a career in the French Diplomatic
> service to solve the problem of providing Valmont with an idle existence.
> They worked out the problem of how to make Valmont and Merteuil have
> the relationship of former mistress and lover who no longer have physical
> relations ... marry them to each other![7]

Unlike all other film versions this one features Prévan, would-be
seducer of Merteuil, but stripped of the novel's plot which has Merteuil
recount the ways in which even a rake to rival Valmont cannot get

the better of her, and reveal how she has him imprisoned on the accusation of attempted rape. Here the Prévan cameo achieves rather more significance by the fact that it is played by Boris Vian, author of the notorious *J'irai cracher sur vos tombes* (*I Spit on your Graves*, 1946). Jazz becomes the soundtrack for this film, emphasising perhaps a youthful, bohemian French culture, making its own moral codes and gradually signifying the abandonment of inhibitions, and Vian's significance as a jazz trumpeter, writer and enthusiast on the French jazz scene, coupled with his notorious novel, and his friendships with Sartre, de Beauvoir and Camus, make him a touchstone of the period in French culture, evoking a heady mixture of philosophy, jazz and the avant garde. Ironically Vian was to die shortly after the making of *Les Liaisons Dangereuses* whilst watching a screening of an adaptation of *J'irai cracher sur vos tombes* (Michel Gast, 1959).[8]

Juliette is shown to be tired of both her current lovers Prévan and American Jerry Court (an obvious play on the name Gercourt from the novel), but is immediately jealous and vengeful when she learns that Court is to be engaged to Valmont's cousin. The rest of the plot is impelled by Juliette's wish for Valmont to seduce Cécile, to which end he follows her on a skiing holiday and literally bumps into Marianne, who (like Tourvel in the novel) is married to a magistrate and is holidaying with an aunt and small child. Cécile's relationship with the young student Danceny takes on a different sexual economy here: although she is a virgin, Cécile is far from the innocent portrayed in the novel. Alone together in his room, Cécile tries to arouse Danceny and yet he treats her like a child and bundles her back to her home so that he can get on with his studies. Perhaps Vadim was inspired by Baudelaire's response to Laclos's novel: 'if this book burns, it can only be as ice burns',[9] given the dominant imagery of fire and snow in the film. Valmont encounters Marianne while skiing, and the snow surrounding her emphasises her purity; Cécile and her friends gaze on approvingly and with obvious desire as Valmont skis down a slope, a dark figure as he cuts through the snow, representing danger and despoilment and the loss of innocence. The path to conquest is thus prepared, and though Cécile protests as Valmont refuses to leave her room (having brought her a tape recorder so that she can listen to messages from Danceny), she is seen as corruptible and actively sexual. Images of snow and fire contrast as the film draws to its climax, and husband and wife plot against each other, using Danceny as their pawn. The party, in this closing scene, contrasts heavily with that of the opening which, although it betrays the capacity of corruption beneath the thin veneer of polite society, by panning the scene and allowing 'overheard' gossiping remarks about Valmont and his young wife, it represents order and propriety, at least on the surface. The final party, which features a live jazz band playing in its midst, becomes more heady and the dancers more agitated; as Valmont and Juliet dramatise their personal conflict, in the background, young women shed more and more clothes and seem to lose their inhibitions to the music (causing Danceny to hastily remove Cécile). In the midst of this chaos, Danceny, returning to the party after discovering Valmont's liaisons with Cécile, physically confronts Valmont, who slips and hits his head on the fire-iron – a close-up focuses on his prone body next to the flickering flames of an open fire and images of hell and damnation are impossible to resist – especially since Juliette, who tries to burn the letters her husband and she have exchanged before the police arrive to investigate his death, accidentally sets her clothes on fire and horribly disfigures her face, summoning up the closing images of the novel where smallpox has destroyed Merteuil's beauty and with it, her sexual power. Marianne becomes unhinged by Valmont's death and it is as if Laclos's preface, imported here as voiceover for the opening of the film, has already shaped this film as a moral modern cautionary tale with its overt symbolism of fire, evil and temptation.

Laclos, it is said, took a great deal of interest in the social position of women, writing essays on women and education that remained unpublished in his lifetime. His portrayal of the female rake, Merteuil, an engaging writing-back at the feminine passivity of *Clarissa*, shows a woman who, by her actions, challenges the view that only men can be sexual opportunists or predators, and also by her own declaration of intent encapsulated in the powerful letter 81, which explains the constraints upon her and the relative freedoms widowhood brings. As Richard Frohock notes, the novel 'presents the complex relations among sex, sadism, gender, and power in notoriously ambiguous terms'.[10] The closure of the novel, as previously mentioned, causes us to speculate over the fates of Valmont and Merteuil and particularly the significance of Valmont's death. Vadim chooses to show Juliette wearing her 'sin' upon her face; Valmont, in the bathos of his accidental death, might be seen as becoming heroic or at least losing some of the stigma attached to his role in the plots hatched by the rakish pair. This centring of the blame on the Merteuil figure becomes a key theme in subsequent adaptations, although there has been debate about how we might interpret Merteuil's actions set against Valmont's, and in particular how we respond to letter 81, which in part anatomises what we see to be the case –Valmont's behaviour is known but this does not prevent him being received in any respectable household, whereas all Merteuil's exploits require utmost secrecy and discretion so that the only person with any documentary evidence of her rakishness is Valmont. As Frohock notes, 'Valmont enjoys augmenting his notoriety, but Merteuil must take all possible precautions to avoid being implicated in any sexual intrigue.'[11] The silence surrounding the scene of Valmont's death is compensated by the letters which circulate around it. In death, it might be argued, Valmont is cleansed; alongside the death of Madame de Tourvel one might characterise the lovers as united again. Merteuil alone, ruined and scarred, upholds society's preference for much harsher depictions of the female sinner, and each adaptation delights in revisiting and reinforcing her demonisation in contrast to Valmont, even when softened by the suggestion that she might be deeply in love with him.

In *Dangerous Liaisons* Merteuil, as in the novel, is booed out of the theatre; her rage and its origins defies singular interpretation; but as she sits at her dressing table and removes her make-up we are reminded of the lengthy establishing shots of the two main characters, which show the elaborate means by which they are dressed, bewigged, powdered and made ready for society. The symbolism needs no further explication and the constant deployment of mirrors and reflecting doors reminds us of the characters' deep self-regard and the collision of being and seeming to be; this does not prevent the communication of deep emotion – not least Valmont's anguished expressions as he faces the mirror in Tourvel's apartments whilst insisting he must break with her because it is 'beyond my control'. Forman's *Valmont* diminishes the punitive focus on Merteuil; but then at the climax of the film the spotlight is gleefully reflected back on those whose belief in society's rectitude is entirely misplaced. Cécile, standing at the altar with Gercourt, cheerfully winks at Madame Rosemonde with whom she has shared the secret that she is carrying Valmont's child; Madame de Tourvel does not die and is seen at the end leaving a flower on his grave. Meanwhile Merteuil looks on at the wedding party ignored by all, in contrast to Danceny, who is surrounded by young women. Valmont is triumphant, but the film ends on the surviving women – particularly Cécile and Madame de Tourvel. Sebastian in *Cruel Intentions* at least expresses some kind of moral doubt when he notes 'we're destroying an innocent girl. You do realise that?' At the end of *Cruel Intentions*, when Annette and Cécile conspire to reproduce copies of Sebastian's journal to hand out to the school congregation at his memorial, this

Valmont, above all, and perhaps because of the teen refunctioning, ironically represents emotional truth and freedom of spirit. His classic car, the subject of his bet with Kathryn, is shown being driven away by Annette, intercut with flashbacks of Sebastian during their courtship and with his journal on the passenger seat. For the first time in the film Annette is wearing sunglasses – the signature accessory of Kathryn and Sebastian – but it is ambiguous as to whether she is taking on their mantle or whether Sebastian's full confession to her (he leaves his journal with her but later is accidentally killed as he saves her from being hit by a car) has purified him. Her driving out of shot represents a journey completed towards adulthood. Just as there is a shock of altered perception when Valmont's and Merteuil's letters are replaced by those of lesser characters after his death in the novel, so the memorial scene in *Cruel Intentions* jolts us back to the knowledge that these characters are children; Kathryn and Annette, back in school uniform, look years younger, and suddenly adults re-emerge into the foreground, altering our perception profoundly. Kathryn's crimes, now displaced on to someone in a kilt and white knee-socks, seem even more unspeakable, and there is little trace of the enduring love between the characters that might be identified in Vadim's, Frears's and Forman's films. Juliette's portrait in Vadim's film depicts her inner evil as she is shown entwined by some kind of thorny creeper, and as Frohock notes, just like the femmes fatales in film noir, the women will get greater punishment.[12] Frears's Merteuil is portrayed as predatory and combative in her statement that 'I was born to dominate your sex and avenge my own', and we are reminded of the militaristic motto declared in Letter 81, that 'one must conquer or die'.[13]

The letters themselves take on a life of their own and the intimacy achieved in this format in the novel is more often replaced in the films by physical proximity. In all cases the written word still makes some kind of more emblematic appearance, alongside other forms of communication such as taped messages and narrative paintings. In *Cruel Intentions*, writing in longhand is Sebastian's great love, because 'emails are for geeks and paedophiles'. In *Untold Scandal* Valmont, the consummate letter-writer, is replaced by Jo-won the artist; his depictions of the trysts he enjoys will become the downfall of Lady Cho at the same time as clandestine communications allow men and women to cross the boundaries of strict segregation. In *Dangerous Liaisons,* where the letters are retained, they are used to powerful effect, such as the scene where we see Valmont writing a letter to Madame de Tourvel on the naked back of a courtesan, so that practically every word he writes takes on a dual meaning. This is emphasised by intercut scenes of Tourvel reading the letter alone and being visibly moved by it; at other times, as Kathryn Carson points out, 'Frears captures the voyeuristic spirit of reading other people's letters by using close camera shots of the actors as they go about eavesdropping and peeping through keyholes.'[14]

Cruel Intentions, Roger Kumble's teen makeover of the novel, works in one contemporary critic's view, because 'Adolescents are, by their nature, heartless, randy and, as all the books inform their frantic parents, eager to test authority's limits.'[15] For Richard Schickel the film works superbly, for adults at least, because we 'may just get a kick out of seeing the little monsters presented as, well, the little monsters they so often are'.[16] In terms of the teenpic genre as a whole and the sub-genre of teen classic adaptations, *Cruel Intentions* was a mould-breaker in the way it maintained all the teen staples but added an edge of sophistication, culture and increased risqué sexual appeal. From its very opening, where it mirrors the classic teenpic establishing shot by having the main character enter the screen in a car, our expectations are thwarted by the fact that Sebastian is driving a Mark 2 Jaguar and going towards New York rather than the playground. The moment of the entrance into school is deferred right up until the end of the film for maximum shock effect, when we are forced to recognise that these unsavoury characters are still children.

Both Kathryn and Sebastian are unlikely teens – given the way they dress, and their frighteningly sophisticated responses to sexual intimacy. Immediately they are visually contrasted with the girlish Cécile, depicted in her first scene wearing a T-shirt with a Koala bear pictured on it and sitting with her legs apart in a skirt so short that her panties can clearly be seen, prompting Sebastian to ask, 'How are things down under?' This child with no sexual knowledge is coldly introduced to their depravity and is seen for the greater part of the film as the pawn of one or the other of them – in a scene which develops hints from the novel, Kathryn encourages Cécile to practise kissing on her: their French kiss is frozen into close-up and reminds us that one implied audience for this film is the teenager exploring his or her own sexual identity, surrounded by explicit and knowing images in our contemporary sexualised culture. In contrast to other teenpics which focus on virginity, friendship cliques and romantic love, *Cruel Intentions* has central protagonists who have no concern for such things and whose only pleasure is in pursuit, manipulation and corruption. As if playing to an audience sated by the standard images of sexual exploration, this film focuses on the more illicit or potentially taboo – not only homoeroticism but oral and anal sexual practices – best exemplified by Kathryn's offer to Sebastian if he wins their wager – 'You can put it anywhere.'

Cruel Intentions shows its legacy to the eighteenth-century novel in intriguing ways and at the same time casts us back to *Dangerous Liaisons* in that even though emphatically not a costume drama, the lavish eighteenth-century furnishings and sophisticated dress of the two lead characters evoke a certain indefinable pastness. At one point Kathryn is wearing a tight bodice which suggests an eighteenth-century corset. New taboos replace those of eighteenth-century French society and Ronald (the Danceny figure) is black; Kathryn and Sebastian have the freedom of mobility of their rakish forebears because their parents are now married to each other and holidaying overseas. The dynamics between the two at times echoes that of *Dangerous Liaisons*, and Sebastian in particular seems to use the same diction and intonation as John Malkovich in his dealings with Cécile; the night after he seduces/ rapes her he makes lewd gestures towards her, just as Malkovich's Valmont does; in another textual homage, Swoosie Kurtz who plays Madame de Volanges in *Dangerous Liaisons* plays Sebastian's analyst in the opening scenes of the film. She becomes distraught when it becomes clear that he, in an act of revenge upon her, has seduced her daughter and posted his exploits on the internet. Another reference to *Dangerous Liaisons* embedded in *Cruel Intentions* is the importance of mirrors, including the car's rear-view mirror and mirrored surfaces, such as sunglasses; just as Malkovich's Valmont only presents his 'real' self to the mirror, Sebastian at one point has to exhort his own reflection to 'get it together, you pussy'. One of Laclos's own intertexts is summoned as Sebastian, having exacted his revenge on his analyst, takes out to lunch the first girl he meets, aptly named Clarissa.

For one critic, at least, the feminist potential of the novel is most clearly located in letter 81 and the subplot which follows Merteuil's thwarting of Prévan's attempts to seduce her, but this is omitted from all the adaptations. In Karen Hollinger's view, 'Crucial to a feminist reading of the novel is its rendering of the Prévan episode as an illustration of Merteuil's attempts to combat the double standard that rendered women subservient to men.'[17] For her both *Dangerous Liaisons* and *Valmont* 'view the novel through the lens of romantic love',[18] particularly in arguably making Merteuil's feelings for Valmont less ambiguous. Star discourse necessarily intrudes on our interpretation of Glenn Close's Merteuil, unavoidably read through the lens of the murderous Alex in *Fatal Attraction*, and adding a taint to her characterisation, a recycling of the implication in the earlier film that all sexually predatory women are unhinged. In both *Cruel Intentions* and *Valmont* it is made clear that Merteuil's ex-lovers have cast her off because of her hysterical intensity, and in this we never lose sight of the fact that these women's revenge narratives are about personal vendetta much more so than Valmont's seemingly motiveless malignity.

For Roz Kaveney, *Cruel Intentions* is 'perhaps the very best of teen films which adapt literary classics', and she adds that 'the genre conventions of the teen film make social ostracism a plausible fear on the part of the protagonists',[19] as does the concern with the value of virginity, which also strikes a further chord after a rash of contemporary teen-focused chastity movements in the United States. The wager itself, as Kaveney also reminds us, is a standard trope in teen adaptations, such as *10 Things I Hate About You* (1999) and *She's All That* (1999). *Cruel Intentions*'s characteristically teenpicky use of contemporary popular music as a soundtrack for the film (and a saleable commodity in its own right, post-release) is only the most obvious use of music in the five adaptations, though in some cases, as in Vadim's use of jazz , it is very striking and emphasises a certain cultural milieu or the identity of the characters themselves. *Cruel Intentions*'s preference for songs with a narrative or message emphasises their homodiegetic engagement. The opening track which accompanies Sebastian's journey into New York is Placebo's 'Every You, Every Me': the repetition of the line ''cos there's nothing else to do' emphasises Sebastian's Generation Y directionlessness from the start. Verve's 'Bitter Sweet Symphony' at the close again offers some homodiegetic engagement: its refrain of 'I can't change' adds a further enigma to Annette's departure and raises the question of whether she has in a sense replaced Sebastian and Kathryn. In addition, as Kaveney notes, this latter song's heavy string sections offer 'a particularly effective blend of the old and the new'.[20]

Cruel Intentions has the distinction of being an accomplished and interesting adaptation and a teenpic which manages to stretch the boundaries of the genre in ways which show a sophisticated engagement with the formula. Not only does the teenpic tap into contemporary adolescent anxieties and curiosities, but it also cements the troubled links between television and film by exporting many TV successes onto film, such as that of Sarah Michelle Gellar, and bringing Ryan Philippe from another teenpic success *I Know What you Did Last Summer* (1997). The year of the film's release, 1999, was also the year in which the Columbine massacre occurred – arguably the most horrifying of a chain of similar events throughout the 1990s and, as Timothy Shary argues, 'Unlike the 1950s, when teen crime was largely exaggerated by Hollywood, the industry could not exaggerate the tragedy of the 1990s murders.'[21] Unlike *Clueless*, which others have criticised as offering essentially a conservative re-evaluation of classic literature at the expense of film, *Cruel Intentions*'s engagement with *Les Liaisons Dangereuses* is a dynamic one: key themes are remodelled to encompass twentieth-century teen life and in the process some elements of the novel are effectively brought to the fore. As Brigitte Humbert notes, 'Kumble is the only director who really picked up Merteuil's subtle but very clear allusions to homosexuality in her encounters with Cécile',[22] and while 'gay' subtexts are an essential part of the knowing teenpic armoury, she is right that the kiss between Kathryn and Cécile echoes Merteuil's letter which tells of Cécile's ripeness for corruption. In a sense the amoral plots of Kathryn and Sebastian most closely resemble the complicated machinations of the two eighteenth-century rakes most winningly, as one is convinced of the potential for teens testing boundaries to give no thought to moral censure or other kinds of reprisals. The setting during the long summer vacation also mimics the aimless wealth of leisure time that we imagine Valmont and Merteuil also share. But what also marks this adaptation apart from other teen adaptations is the extent to which these two are apart from their peers – they're not simply the Goths among glamour girls, or the immensely wealthy or girl from the wrong side of the tracks, but actually seem to have no teen characteristics at all. Their dress is timeless designer contemporary and they are shown inhabiting their parents' Manhattan apartment in their absence as if they were already responsible adults.

Kathryn always, as she laments, gets dumped in favour of the 'innocent little twits', so perhaps at the back of this finale with its overt revenge of the good girls there is a feminist subtext lurking more energetically than first appears. Sebastian, while cyber-literate, as shown by his exploits at the beginning of the film, has a love of writing in more traditional formats; further, writing via his journal comes to represent truth and authentic emotion set against Annette's manifesto in favour of virginity, published in a magazine, which comes to be seen as a shield for her own lack of emotional and sexual engagement with her previous boyfriend. For those who find the teenpic form a sad indictment of the American mass market because 'without the support of the teenage audience, few theatrical movies break even, fewer still become hits, and none become blockbusters',[23] this is an example of one which works at least on a double register and offers a sophisticated engagement with the process of adaptation as well as with the means by which one successful film (*Dangerous Liaisons*) can be recentred as 'origin' to which the use of Laclos adds further narrative engagement and sexual titillation.

Valmont, as the name suggests, focuses more unambiguously on Valmont's exploits as a seducer, with Merteuil taking the back seat as a sexy, vengeful but unlikeable opponent who is denounced as possibly mentally unstable by her lover Gercourt as he moves towards his arranged marriage with Cécile. This Cécile, in common with Selma Blair's performance in *Cruel Intentions*, looks convincingly and disturbingly like a teenager. Indeed, so wide-eyed and innocent is this Cécile (Fairuza Balk, aged 14 at the time of filming) that she is deliberately figured much more as a child than as a young woman in the opening establishing scenes, recalling the naïve and bland (and accordingly dull) letters from her to her friend which begin the novel. Valmont's engagement with her until the 'seduction' is as an older brother or uncle. As the company assemble for a picnic in the grounds, Valmont (Colin Firth) mock duels with Cécile, not only prefiguring the bathos of his final drunken duel with Danceny, but emphasising Danceny's prowess with the sword in a previous interpolated scene that has him trying out for Gercourt's regiment. Most significantly the scene increases our sense of shock at his ability to rape/seduce the same child in ensuing scenes. As noted earlier, this is an adaptation which has Valmont at the centre and all the women as satellites around him – a scene shows him dancing with the key female characters (including his aunt, the elderly Madame Rosemonde) in a way which emphasises their own personalities and the distinctiveness of his relationship with each of them. The musical score emphasises this as they all have their own musical tropes associated with them – the most melancholy being that of Madame de Tourvel. Once Valmont dies, the emphasis appears to be on the cyclical nature of male rakery, with the young Danceny featured in the wings at Cécile's wedding ceremony to Gercourt, surrounded by admiring young women, whereas Merteuil is friendless, suggesting her sexual allure is on the wane.

Untold Scandal once again balances its homage to Laclos with a more obvious one to *Dangerous Liaisons*. In common with this latter film it maintains the novel's historical location but shifts the setting to eighteenth-century Korea. Colour figures as a central symbolic web in the film, underpinned also by the importance of flowers and the bright primary colours Jo-won uses in his paintings (the metaphorical replacement to the letters, in that it is these that are circulated and used to disgrace Lady Cho at the climax). As in the films of the Japanese director Akira Kurosawa, which interpolate Western literary classics such as *King Lear* in *Ran,* the landscape at times seems to dwarf human activity and concerns and the narrative takes on a more romantic and poetic tone. Jo-won's flight to reunite with Suk after he is attacked and stabbed is long and touchingly beautiful while being chillingly stark. The bleeding body of Jo-won clings limply to his servant as he rides behind him across a spectacular beach, his white robes stained with blood which drips on to the sand. Once his death is reported to Suk she wears the red scarf that he gave to her and slowly walks over a frozen lake. As the ice gives way and she sinks under the water all that is left is this trace of red on white, recalling both the bloodstained body of Jo-won and also the memorable aerial shot in the penultimate scene of *Dangerous Liaisons* where Valmont's body, sprawled in the snow, is shaded by a trail of blood which suggests vividly his violent death; Annette in *Cruel Intentions* is dressed entirely in white as she leaves her house to find Sebastian who will moments later be killed by a car as he saves her: there is no blood in view, but the lining of his coat which spreads about him is a deep red. As much as *Cruel Intentions* and *Untold Scandal* visually recall the stunning shot of Valmont's death in *Dangerous Liaisons*, symbolically the three films summon again the imagery of fire and ice deployed in Vadim's adaptation. The crane shot which removes us from narrative intimacy with Valmont at the point of his death in *Dangerous Liaisons* itself pays homage to that moment of narrative dislocation in Laclos's novel, when the letters from Valmont abruptly cease.

One debate which often retreats to the background in comparative adaptation critiques is that of quality: how is one to assess a 'good' adaptation when all these adaptations offer something different, even if three can be broadly grouped under a 'costume drama' category and three are an updating or transposition event (assuming *Untold Scandal* counts twice as both a costume drama and cultural transposition)? It is quite often easy to assume that the teen makeover offers something dramatic or radical to the process of adaptation, but each of these versions intervenes in Laclos's text to emerge with something new. Moreover, *Dangerous Liaisons*, easily the most commercially successful adaptation of the five, becomes itself a hypotext to be reckoned with.

Conclusion: Impure Cinema – Another Apology for Adaptations

This book is subtitled *Impure Cinema* in order to call attention to the bad press that adaptations have received since the beginning of film's history and, like every new and consequently aesthetically questionable art form, the book offers another 'apology'. The initial reaction to any emerging form of entertainment is often to dismiss it as rubbish, seeing it as a throwback to what went before, and whilst apologists, since and before the likes of Sir Philip Sidney, have won their debates about the artistic merits of their beloved art forms, in spite of a history that spans over one hundred years, the jury still seems to be out on the merit of adaptations. This book has tried to chart the gradual recognition of cineastes and literary scholars to the aesthetic challenges of the adaptation guided by Bazin's repudiation of the concept of the author as offering a way through the Scylla and Charybdis of Film and Literary Studies.

The book has touched upon the history of attitudes to adaptations and a variety of adaptations themselves, from a seemingly authorless text (*Peter Pan*), to an adaptation of a popular novel that is fundamentally an adaptation of a film (*Star Wars* as ur-text to *Harry Potter and the Philosopher's Stone*). The final three chapters reflect on the genrification of Shakespeare and Austen, anti-classic adaptations of nineteenth-century canonical novels, and five adaptations of a quintessentially writerly novel, *Les Liaisons Dangereuses*.

In the first issue of the journal, *Adaptation,* we tried (with our co-editor, Timothy Corrigan) to account for the exclusion of film adaptations from the beginning of the twentieth century from the emergent field of Film Studies and the established area of literature, and came up with a variety of reasons. Cineastes at the beginning of the twentieth century resented film's reliance on literature, believing film should stand on its own feet; writers and literary scholars felt that film devalued and desecrated literature and that bringing culture 'to the masses' could therefore potentially destroy 'culture' altogether; the arrival of Film Studies in the 1960s, often within English departments, was greeted with a mixed response, often berated as not a 'real' subject, and those who championed it stayed clear of adaptations of literary texts, possibly in order to remove themselves from their literary colleagues, as a way of ensuring the autonomy of their own subject; logocentricism, or a belief in the primacy of the written word, has prevailed, resulting in unfavourable comparisons between film and book in which the book always wins; prejudice that you can't mix art with money has persisted; the notion that there has to be a single author in order for a work to be regarded as art has not gone away, especially in literary circles; the idea that an adaptation can only be a copy of a literary text has resulted in the form being regarded in an inferior light; 'adaptation' is often a derogatory term, the form is frequently associated with emotive words such as 'desecrate', 'ransack' or 'betray', sometimes even analogous with 'failure'. When a film is based on a canonical text, such as *Hamlet* or *Pride and Prejudice*, it's virtually impossible to 'triumph' over its original, whereas when it adapts a lesser known text, it often ceases to be an adaptation and becomes, for most viewers, the 'original'; and finally, adaptations have been interpreted as having a single 'source' text, other cinematic and cultural contexts are often swept aside.[1]

Each of the above, no doubt more, deserves a book-length study of its own. Taking the above suggestions as to why it has taken so long for adaptations to be recognised in literary, film and cultural studies, we can identify at least as many areas for further study. The impact of the hostility to adaptations for contaminating cinema has been discussed in Chapter 3. Cineastes' repudiation of adaptations can be further evaluated by uncovering film reviews and filmmakers' own reflections on the use of literary texts as a narrative basis. The field is crying out for an evaluation of the legacy of the prejudice to adaptations in the early period of cinema, a prejudice that possibly peaked with the introduction of sound (See Deborah Cartmell, 'Adaptation and the Coming of Sound').[2] The late arrival of film in literary studies and the consequent effect upon the English curriculum deserve further scrutiny, especially as the employment of film material in English essays and articles is, even now, a taboo in some circles. The severance of Film Studies from Literary Studies has meant that adaptations have been pushed to the margins of both subjects to the degree that it is no longer fashionable to use the word 'literature'. While certain adaptation scholars have excluded the literary text from their analysis of adaptations, the slow and often painful death of literature in the field needs to be either better defended or refuted (see Christine Geraghty, *Now a Major*

Motion Picture: Film Adaptations of Literature and Drama).[3] Work on
the phenomenon of the novelisation, novels that have as their primary
source, a film, and novels that are written with a primary motive of
being turned into films, could be expanded (see Jan Baetens, 'From
Screen to Text: Novelization, the Hidden Continent').[4] The economic
condition of the adaptation's production is an area that is now gaining
some momentum – scholars have almost always sought and/or preferred to isolate artistic rather than economic reasons for the choices
made in film adaptation (see Simone Murray, 'Phantom Adaptations:
Eucalyptus, the Adaptation Industry and the Film That Never Was').[5]
The fragmentation of authorship to include actors, casting, cinematography, sound, costume, music and the numerous other components
that contribute to an adaptation has gradually replaced the 'author'
and 'auteur' approach to adaptations (see Geraghty, *Now a Major
Motion Picture: Film Adaptations of Literature and Drama*).[6] Clearly,
the defects of 'fidelity criticism' are something almost all scholars of
adaptations now take for granted, but the quest for fidelity is still the
knee-jerk reaction of uninitiated students and journalists. The contemporary media perception of what constitutes an adaptation is an
area that could be opened up and publicly refuted (see Thomas Leitch,
*Film Adaptation and its Discontents: From Gone with the Wind to the
Passion of the Christ*).[7] Even the champion of the adaptation, André
Bazin, without qualification, uses labels like 'impure', possibly unintentionally detracting from his overall argument. We need to look more
closely at the critical vocabulary associated with adaptation studies.
Adaptations of popular and lesser known novels, or adaptations that
have become the originals in the minds of the majority of their audience, is another area worthy of book-length study. The literary 'source'
as intertext is an approach aired by most contemporary scholars, but
it may be worth pausing and reflecting upon how far we can or should
diminish the 'literary' (see Linda Hutcheon, *A Theory of Adaptation*
and Thomas Leitch, *Film Adaptation and its Discontents: From Gone
with the Wind to the Passion of the Christ*).[8]

Shelley Cobb has taken the point about the unfortunate language
associated with adaptations for further consideration in a feminist
critique of fidelity, reflecting on the deeply gendered language of
adaptation criticism, a language that implicitly identifies the text as
a chaste woman whose honour demands defence.[9] Bluestone himself
engages in such a linguistic tactic, often defending 'liberties' taken by
filmmakers as reflecting authorial intentions: as if the text is a woman
who secretly 'wants it'. In the case of *Pride and Prejudice* (1940), the

film 'serves' the book by opening it up to new possibilities, consistent with Austen's 'own intentions':

> But that they [the filmmakers] should come so close to the image Jane Austen had in mind, providing Kitty with the affable Denny (if not her clergyman), and Mary with the gentle Mr. Witherington, indicates a remarkable power of projection into Jane Austen's artistic sensibility.[10]

And it serves the author by selling her book to a new generation of readers:

> Yet, in another way, the film may have had a more extensive influence than even the film-makers are aware. In June, 1940, in direct response to the film's premier, Pocket Books brought out a soft-cover edition of *Pride and Prejudice*. By 1948, just eight years late, Jane Austen's novel had gone into twenty-one printings.[11]

The film 'serves' the book just as Darcy gallantly serves Elizabeth, unexpectedly and generously offering the author a Pemberley that meets entirely with her approval. While Bluestone adopts the language of courtly love, other critics see the film as seducer, corrupter and rapist. Among the many examples we could cite, John Patterson, writing for the *Guardian,* sees a beloved book as if it were now a degraded lover; the adaptation, *Love in the Time of Cholera* (2007), 'captures not one single sniff of the intoxicating perfumes of that beloved masterpiece', and while watching the film Patterson imagines the hearts of millions of readers 'breaking in two'.[12] According to Patterson, television series such as *The Wire* and *The Sopranos* are masterpieces in ways in which an adaptation of, say, Jane Austen, can never be:

> If today you want to sink your teeth into the kind of rich, vivid triple-decker Victorian state-of-the-nation, weekly-serial novel that depicts society from top to bottom in all its colour and depravity, don't bother with *Vanity Fair* or *Bleak House*. Just buy a box set of *The Wire* or *The Sopranos* – bottomless works of art that are not based on novels.[13]

The term 'impure' also has unfortunate associations, no doubt the reason Hugh Gray, Bazin's translator, changed the title of this groundbreaking essay from 'Pour un Cinéma Impur: Défence de l'adaptation' to 'In Defense of Mixed Cinema', while in the most recent translation into English, the word 'impure' has returned to Bazin's essay.[14] Bazin's use of the adjective *impur* has unfortunately covertly stuck to the field of adaptations, tainting it with the assumption that it's neither one thing nor the other, a hybrid, mongrel, crossbreed;

depending upon the perspective, the film or the novel has become tainted and has 'bad blood' as a result of an unnatural and/or forced union. Historically, when it has come to adaptations, critics on both sides of the film and literature fence have unknowingly descended into not just a gendered, but an unintentionally racialist discourse, assuming that impurity or hybridity is a defect rather than a virtue. Even the staunchest defenders, such as Bazin himself, sometimes employ a language that is adaptation studies' own worst enemy. Admitting that there are good and bad adaptations, he writes: 'There are fruitful cross-breedings which add to the qualities derived from the parents; there are attractive but barren hybrids and there are likewise hideous combinations that bring forth nothing but chimeras.'[15] Unlike critics who view adaptation in the Darwinian sense of an evolutionary selection that takes the best from both worlds, Bazin's terminology unfortunately condemns it to the outcome of unregulated experiments in cross-breeding, sometimes producing new and more powerful organisms, while sometimes resulting in Frankensteinian genetic engineering, gone disastrously wrong. Since the beginning of its history, terminology has dogged the field of adaptations, reflected in its many names, among them, 'picturisations', 'impure cinema', 'mixed cinema', 'literary cinema', 'literature on screen' and finally, the most neutral to date and possibly the most nondescript of all: 'adaptations'.

Rather than trying to pin it down, we have tried to identify the well-intentioned but inevitably doomed attempts to systematically categorise as a means of escaping simple and unprofitable comparisons between book and film. Not meaning to fall into the numerous pitfalls of political correctness, this study aims to celebrate diversity, claiming to only touch upon the manifold approaches that a field, that has hybridity at its very heart, can yield.

Notes

Introduction

1. 'The Bankruptcy of Cinema as Art', in *The Movies on Trial: The Views and Opinions of Outstanding Personalities: Screen Entertainment Past and Present*, ed. William J. Perlman, New York: Macmillan, 1936, pp. 113–40, pp. 134–5.
2. *The Cambridge Companion to Literature on Screen*, ed. Deborah Cartmell and Imelda Whelehan, Cambridge: Cambridge University Press, 2007.
3. *Adaptations: From Text to Screen, Screen to Text*, ed. Deborah Cartmell and Imelda Whelehan, London: Routledge, 1999, pp. 3–19.
4. See Introduction, *Rethinking the Novel/Film Debate*, Cambridge: Cambridge University Press, 2003, pp. 1–8.
5. 'The Cinema', in *The Captain's Death Bed and Other Essays*, London: Hogarth Press, 1950, pp. 160–71, p. 166.
6. William Hunter, *Scrutiny of Cinema*, London: Wishart & Co., 1932, p. 9. This is an expanded version of 'The Art Form of Democracy' that appeared in *Scrutiny* 1(1), 1932, 61–5.
7. 'Logocentricism' throughout the book is used in the general sense that the word is central.
8. 'Introduction: The Theory and Practice of Adaptation', in *Literature and Film: A Guide to the Theory and Practice of Film Adaptation*, ed. Robert Stam and Alessandra Raengo, Malden, MA and Oxford: Blackwell, 2005, pp. 1–52, pp. 3–8.
9. Ibid., p. 41.
10. *The Novel and the Cinema*, Rutherford, NJ: Fairleigh Dickinson University Press, 1975, p. 222.
11. John Brannigan, *New Historicism and Cultural Materialism*, Basingstoke: Macmillan, 1998, p. 97.
12. Again, we are indebted to Robert Stam for his extremely lucid reading and application of Genette's concept of 'transtextuality' in *Literature and Film*, pp. 26–31.
13. LeRoy was producer on this film.
14. 'Adaptation: the Genre', in *Adaptation*, 1(2), 2008, 106–20.

1   Adaptations: Theories, Interpretations and New Dilemmas

1. Imelda Whelehan, 'Adaptations: the Contemporary Dilemmas', in Deborah Cartmell and Imelda Whelehan, eds., *Adaptations: From Text to Screen, Screen to Text*, London: Routledge, 1999, p. 4.

2. Linda Hutcheon, *A Theory of Adaptation*, New York: Routledge, 2006, p. 27.
3. Ibid., p. 28.
4. Rebecca Housel, *From Camera Lens to Critical Lens: A Collection of Best Essays on Film Adaptation*, Newcastle: Cambridge Scholars Press, 2006, p. xi.
5. Thomas Leitch, *Film Adaptation and its Discontents: From 'Gone with the Wind' to 'The Passion of the Christ'* Baltimore: Johns Hopkins University Press, 2007, p. 4.
6. Ibid., p. 5.
7. *Now a Major Motion Picture: Film Adaptations of Literature and Drama*, Lanham, MD: Rowman & Littlefield, 2008, p. 1.
8. Ibid., p. 4.
9. See for example the argument outlined in David Kranz and Nancy Mellerski's Introduction to their recent edited collection, *In/Fidelity: Essays on Film Adaptation*, Newcastle: Cambridge Scholars Press, 2008, pp. 1–11.
10. Robert Stam, 'The Theory and Practice of Adaptation', in Robert Stam and Alessandra Raengo, eds., *Literature and Film: A Guide to the Theory and Practice of Film Adaptation*, Oxford: Blackwell, 2005, p. 3.
11. Ibid., p. 46.
12. In Robert B. Ray, *How a Film Theory Got Lost and Other Mysteries in Cultural Studies*, Bloomington: Indiana University Press, 2001.
13. Geraghty, *Now a Major Motion Picture*, p. 11.
14. Jonathan Gray, *Watching the Simpsons: Television, Parody, and Intertextuality*, New York: Routledge, 2006, p. 34.
15. See *Pulping Fictions* (1996), *Trash Aesthetics* (1997), *Sisterhoods* (1998), *Alien Identities* (1999), *Classics in Film and Fiction* (2000), ed. Deborah Cartmell, I.Q. Hunter, Heidi Kaye and Imelda Whelehan and *Retrovisions*, ed. Deborah Cartmell, I.Q. Hunter and Imelda Whelehan (2001), all London: Pluto Press.
16. Jonathan Gray, *Watching the Simpsons: Television, Parody, and Intertextuality*, p. 31.
17. Bruce R. Burningham, 'Walt Disney's *Toy Story* as Postmodern *Don Quixote*', *Cervantes: Bulletin of the Cervantes Society of America*, 20(1), 2000, 157–74. Thanks to Nic Felton for drawing our attention to this.
18. Gérard Genette, *Paratexts: Thresholds of Interpretation* (trans. Jane E. Lewin, Foreword, Richard Macksey), Cambridge: Cambridge University Press, 1997 (first pub in French, 1987), p. 2.
19. Ibid., p. 5.
20. See Simone Murray, 'Phantom Adaptations: *Eucalyptus*, the adaptation industry and the film that never was', *Adaptation*, 1(1), 2008, 5–23.
21. Kate Ellis and E. Ann Kaplan (with postscript by Kaplan) 'Feminism in Bronte's *Jane Eyre* and its Film Versions', ed. Barbara Tepa Lupack, *Nineteenth Century Women at the Movies: Adapting Classic Women's*

Fiction to Film, Bowling Green, OH: Bowling Green State University Popular Press, 1999, p. 205.

22. Dudley Andrew, 'The Well-Worn Muse: Adaptation in Film History and Theory', in *Prose Fiction*, ed. Syndy M. Conger and Janice R. Welsch, Macomb: Western Illinois University Press, 1980, pp. 11–17, p. 12.
23. Robin Swicord, 'Under the Skin: Adapting Novels for the Screen' in *In/ Fidelity: Essays on Film Adaptation*, ed. Kranz and Mellerski, p. 20.
24. Kranz and Mellerski, p. 4.
25. Andrew, 'The Well-Worn Muse,' p. 16.
26. Geoffrey Wagner, *The Novel and the Cinema* (Rutherford, NJ: Fairleigh Dickinson University Press, 1975), p. 222.
27. *Criticism,* 45(2), 2003, 149–71.
28. For the conversation see 'A Practical Understanding of Literature on Screen: Two Conversations with Andrew Davies', in *The Cambridge Companion to Literature on Screen,* ed. Deborah Cartmell and Imelda Whelehan, Cambridge: Cambridge University Press', pp. 239–51.
29. 'Introduction: Film and the Reign of Adaptation', in *Film Adaptation*, ed. James Naremore, London: Athlone Press, 2000, p. 9.
30. *Film Adaptation*, ed. Naremore, p. 15.
31. André Bazin, 'Adaptation, or the Cinema as Digest', ibid., p. 26.
32. Robert B. Ray, 'The Field of "Literature and Film"', in *Film Adaptation*, ed. Naremore, p. 38.
33. Ibid., p. 40.
34. Robert Stam, 'Beyond Fidelity: The Dialogics of Adaptation' in *Film Adaptation*, ed. Naremore, p. 59.
35. Keith Cohen, *Film and Fiction: The Dynamics of Exchange*, New Haven, CT: Yale University Press, 1979, p. 210.
36. Hutcheon, *Theory of Adaptation*, p. 107.
37. Ibid., p. 114.
38. Ibid., p. 118.
39. Ibid., p. 122.
40. Robert Stam, 'The Theory and Practice of Adaptation', in *Literature and Film: A Guide to the Theory and Practice of Film Adaptation,* p. 7.

2 Film on Literature: Film as the New Shakespeare

1. Deborah Cartmell, 'The Shakespeare on Screen Industry', in *Adaptations: From Text to Screen, Screen to Text*, ed. Deborah Cartmell and Imelda Whelehan, London and New York: Routledge, 1999, pp. 29–37.
2. Some material in this chapter appears in Deborah Cartmell, 'Film as the New Shakespeare and Film on Shakespeare: Reversing the Shakespeare/ Film Trajectory', *Literature Compass*, 3(5), 2006, 1150–9.
3. Allardyce Nicoll, *Film and Theatre,* London: Harrap, 1936, p. 33.
4. *Scrutiny of Cinema,* London: Wishart, 1932, p. 50.

5. Margaret Farrand Thorp (1939), quoted in George Bluestone, *Novels into Films*, Berkeley, Los Angeles and London: University of California Press, 1973, p. 44

6. 'Adaptation, or the Cinema as Digest' (1948), in *Film Adaptation*, ed. James Naremore, London: Athlone, 2000, pp. 19–17, p. 23.

7. *The Rehearsal from Shakespeare to Sheridan*, Oxford: Clarendon, 2000, pp. 94–8.

8. *Film and Theatre*, p. 30.

9. *Film and Theatre*, pp. 122–3.

10. 'Literature and Cinema: Reply to a Questionnaire' (1928), in *Eisenstein: Writings 1922–1934*, London and Bloomington: BFI and Indiana University Press, 1988, pp. 95–9, p. 99.

11. 'Cinema and the Classics' (1933), in *Eisenstein: Writings*, p. 276.

12. 'Dickens, Griffiths and the Film Today' (1944), in *Film Form*, ed. Jay Leyda, London: Dennis Dobson, 1963, pp. 195–256, p. 213.

13. *Film Form*, pp. 211–17. For a detailed account of Dickens's proto-cinematic style, see Grahame Smith, *Dickens and the Dream of Cinema*, Manchester: Manchester University Press, 2003.

14. *Film Form*, p. 213.

15. Luke McKernan, 'A Scene – *King John* – Now Playing at Her Majesty's Theatre', in *Moving Performance: British Stage and Screen, 1890s to 1920s*, ed. Linda Fitzimmons and Sarah Street, Trowbridge: Flicks, 2000, pp. 56–68, p. 59.

16. W. Uricchio and R.E. Pearson, *Reframing Culture: The Case of the Vitagraph Quality Films*, Princeton: Princeton University Press, 1993, p. 48.

17. *The Devil's Camera: 1894–1940*, London: Epworth Press, 1932, p. 20.

18. *The Devil's Camera*, p. 101.

19. '*Romeo and Juliet*' (1936), in *Graham Greene on Film: Collected Film Criticism 1935–1940*, ed. John Russell Taylor, New York: Simon & Schuster, 1973, p. 111.

20. '*Romeo and Juliet*', p. 111

21. Nicoll, *Film and Theatre*, p. 42.

22. 'The Sound Film: Salvation of Cinema' (1929), in *Close Up: Cinema and Modernism*, ed. James Donald, Anne Friedberg and Laura Marcus, London: Cassell, 1998, pp. 87–8, p. 87.

23. *Scrutiny of Cinema*, p. 50

24. Ibid., p. 50.

25. *The Social History of Art. Four: Naturalism, Impressionism, The Film Age* (1951); rpt. London: Routledge & Kegan Paul, 1962, p. 239.

26. Ibid., p. 240.

27. Herbert Read, *A Coat of Many Colours: Occasional Essays*, London: George Routledge & Sons, 1945, p. 230.

28. 'In Defense of Mixed Cinema', in *What is Cinema?*, ed. Hugh Gray, Berkeley and London: University of California Press, 1971, pp. 53–75. See

discussion of 'mixed cinema' in Dudley Andrew, *André Bazin*, New York: Oxford University Press, 1978, pp. 182–7.

29. 'Reading Film and Literature', in *The Cambridge Companion to Literature on Screen*, ed. Deborah Cartmell and Imelda Whelehan, Cambridge: Cambridge University Press, 2007, pp. 15–28.

30. *Adaptation and Appropriation*, London and New York: Routledge, 2006, p. 9.

31. 'Gospel Narratives on Silent Film', in *The Cambridge Companion to Literature on Screen*, pp. 47–60, p. 58.

32. See Ann Thompson and Neil Taylor's note in their edition of *Hamlet*, London: Thomson Learning, 2006, p. 309. All quotations from *Hamlet* are taken from this edition.

33. From an unpublished filmography of *Hamlet* by Luke McKernan, cited by Ann Thompson, 'Asta Nielsen and the Mystery of *Hamlet*', in *Shakespeare the Movie: Popularizing the Plays on Film, TV and Video*, ed. Lynda E. Boose and Richard Burt, London and New York: Routledge, 1997, pp. 215–24, p. 217.

34. ' "Sir J. and Lady Forbes-Robertson left for America on Saturday": Marketing the 1913 *Hamlet* for Stage and Screen', in *Moving Performance: British Stage and Screen 1890s–1920s*, pp. 44–55.

35. Luke McKernan and Olwen Terris, eds., *Walking Shadows: Shakespeare in the National Film and Television Archives*, London: BFI, 1994, p. 47.

36. Kenneth Rothwell, *A History of Shakespeare on Screen*, Cambridge: Cambridge University Press, 1999, p. 21.

37. Robert Hamilton Ball, *Shakespeare on Silent Film: A Strange and Eventful History*, London: George Allen & Unwin, 1968, p. 278.

38. Ann Thompson and Neil Taylor, *Hamlet*, p. 101.

39. Jack Jorgens, *Shakespeare on Film*, Bloomington: Indiana University Press, 1977, pp. 7–35.

40. Robert Shaughnessy, 'Theatricality: Stage, Screen and Nation: *Hamlet* and the Space of History', in *A Concise Companion to Shakespeare on Screen*, Oxford: Blackwell, 2006, pp. 54–76.

3   Literature on Film: Writers on Adaptations in the Early Twentieth Century

1. 'The Cinema', in *The Captain's Death Bed and Other Essays*, London: Hogarth Press, 1950, pp. 160–71, p. 168.

2. Ibid., p. 166.

3. Charles Davy, *Footnotes to the Film*, London: Lovat Dickson, 1937, p. 316.

4. *Collected Poems, 1912–1944*, ed. Louis L. Martz, New York: New Directions, 1983. See also Susan McCabe, *Cinematic Modernism: Modernist Poetry and Film*, Cambridge: Cambridge University Press, 2005.

5. Vachel Lindsay, from *The Art of the Moving Picture*, 1915; rev. 1922, reprinted in *Film and Literature: An Introduction and Reader*, ed. Timothy Corrigan (1999 rpt. Englewood Cliffs, NJ: Prentice Hall, 2000), p. 100.
6. Joseph Conrad, *A Conrad Argosy*, New York, 1942, p. 83.
7. As noted by Joy Gould Boyum, *Double Exposure: Fiction into Film*, New York: New American Library, 1985, p. 3.
8. A discussion of the 'movie novel' can be found in Robert Richardson, *Literature and Film*, Bloomington and London: Indiana University Press, 1973, and for further titles and synopses see Nancy Brooker-Bowers, *The Hollywood Novel and Other Novels about Film, 1912–1982*, New York: Garland, 1985.
9. Nathanael West, *The Day of the Locust*, New York: Buccaneer Books, 1939, pp. 99–100.
10. Charles Musser, 'The Devil's Parody: Horace McCoy's Appropriation and Refiguration of Two Hollywood Musicals', in *A Companion to Literature and Film*, ed. Robert Stam and Alessandra Raengo, Oxford: Blackwell, 2004, p. 247.
11. *The Last Tycoon*, 1941, 1960; rpt. London and New York: Penguin, 2001, p. 5.
12. 'Subjects and Stories', in *Footnotes to the Film*, ed. Charles Davy, London and Toronto: Lovat Dickson, 1937, pp. 57–71.
13. See Gene D. Philips and John C. Tibbetts, 'Appendix: Scenes from a Hollywood Life: The Novelist as Screenwriter', in *Novels into Film*, ed. John C. Tibbetts and James M. Welsh, 1998, 2nd ed. New York: Facts on File, 2005, pp. 517–21.
14. Quoted in *Novels into Film*, ed. Tibbetts and Welsh, p. 517.
15. *Brave New World*, London: Vintage, 2004, p. 145.
16. 'Silence is Golden', in *Authors on Film*, ed. Harry Geduld, Bloomington and London: Indiana University Press, 1972, p. 73.
17. See Virginia M. Clark, *Aldous Huxley and Film*, Metuchen, NJ and London: Scarecrow Press, 1984.
18. Quoted in John M. Desmond and Peter Hawkes, *Adaptation: Studying Film and Literature*, Boston: McGraw Hill, 2006, p. 96.
19. Béla Balázs, *Theory of the Film: Character and Growth of a New Art* (trans. from Hungarian by Edith Bone), New York: Dover Publications, 1970, p. 18. [The first Hungarian edition was in 1948 and this edition is based on the first English translation of 1952.]
20. 'Class-Consciousness and the Movies', *Atlantic Monthly*, 115, 1915, 48–56, p. 55.
21. 'Sacred Word, Profane Image: Theologies of Adaptation,' in *A Companion to Literature and Film*, ed. Stam and Raengo, pp. 92–111, p. 92.
22. Richard Schickel, *The Disney Version*, New York: Avon Books, 1968, p. 191.
23. *What is Literature?*, trans. Bernard Frechtman, London: Methuen, 1967; French edn 1948, p. 181.

24. *The Mechanized Muse*, London: George Allen & Unwin, 1942, p. 48.
25. Ibid., p. 25.
26. Ibid., p. 49.
27. Barton Rascoe, *Bookman*, 54(3), 1921, 193–9, p. 196.
28. Ibid., p. 197.
29. 'The Drama, the Theatre and the Films: A Dialogue between Bernard Shaw and Archibald Henderson, his Biographer', *Fortnightly Review*, 693, 1 September 1924, 289–302, p. 290.
30. Ibid., p. 292.
31. 'The Course of Realism', in *Footnotes to the Film*, ed. Charles Davy, London: Lovat Dickson, 1937, pp. 137–61, pp. 139–40.
32. B. Clayton, 'Shakespeare and the Talkies', *English Review*, 44 (1929), 739–52, p. 739.
33. *Scrutiny*, I(1), 1932, 61–5, p. 62.
34. Ibid., p. 61.
35. *Scrutiny of Cinema*, London: Wishart, 1932, p. 9.
36. Ibid., p. 11.
37. The New York survey is cited in Desmond and Hawkes, *Adaptation*, p. 15.
38. Herbert Francis Sherwood, 'Democracy and the Movies', *Bookman*, 47 (1918), 235–9, p. 237.
39. 'The Drama, the Theatre and the Films', *Fortnightly Review*, 693, 292.
40. 'Subjects and Stories', in *Footnotes to the Film*, ed. Charles Davy, London and Toronto: Lovat Dickson, 1937, pp. 57–71, p. 64.
41. André Bazin, 'In Defense of Mixed Cinema', in *What is Cinema?* essays trans. and selected by Hugh Gray, forewords by Jean Renoir and Dudley Andrew, Vol. 1, Berkeley: University of California Press, 2005, p. 66.
42. *Novels into Film: The Metamorphoses of Fiction into Cinema*, Berkeley: University of California Press, 1975, p. 62.
43. Ibid., p. 43.
44. A notable exception to this is Timothy Corrigan, *Film and Literature*, Englewood Cliffs, NJ: Prentice Hall, 2000.
45. The following material on the growth of Shakespeare on screen is an expansion of Deborah Cartmell, 'The Shakespeare on Screen Industry', in *Adaptations*, ed. Deborah Cartmell and Imelda Whelehan, London and New York: Routledge, 1999, pp. 29–37.
46. *How a Film Theory Got Lost and Other Mysteries in Cultural Studies*, Princeton: Princeton University Press, 1985, pp. 120–31.
47. See *Literature through Film: Realism, Magic, and the Art of Adaptation*, Malden and Oxford: Blackwell, 2005, p. 5.
48. *Rethinking the Novel/Film Debate*, Cambridge: Cambridge University Press, 2003.
49. 1 November 1940.
50. http://film.guardian.co.uk/features/featurepages/0,4120,1583760,00.html 21/11/05.

51. *Shakespearean Negotiations*, Princeton: Princeton University Press, 1988, p. 1.
52. Boyum, *Double Exposure: Fiction into Film*, p. 15.
53. Richard Maltby, '"To Prevent the Prevalent Type of Book": Censorship and Adaptation in Hollywood, 1924–1934', in *Film Adaptation*, ed. James Naremore, New Brunswick, NJ: Rutgers University Press, 2000, p. 80.
54. Brian McFarlane, *Novel to Film: An Introduction to the Theory of Adaptation*, Oxford: Oxford University Press, 1996, p. 6.
55. Robert Stam, 'Beyond Fidelity: The Dialogics of Adaptation', in *Film Adaptation*, ed. James Naremore, p. 54.
56. Stam , p. 64.
57. 'Which Shakespeare to Love? Film, Fidelity, and the Performance of Literature', in *High-Pop: Making Culture into Popular Entertainment*, ed. Jim Collins, Oxford: Blackwell, 2002, p. 158.
58. 'Introduction', in Collins, *High-Pop*, pp. 1–2.
59. ' Introduction', in *Film Adaptation*, ed. Naremore, p. 15.
60. Robert B. Ray, 'The Field of "Literature and Film"', in *Film Adaptation*, ed. Naremore, p. 42.
61. Ibid., p. 46.
62. *A Theory of Adaptation*, London and New York: Routledge, 2006, p. 17.
63. *Film Adaptation and its Discontents*, Baltimore: Johns Hopkins University Press, 2007, p. 302.

4 Authorial Suicide: Adaptation as Appropriation in *Peter Pan*

1. For an account of this film, see Denis MacKail, *The Story of J.M.B*, London: Peter Davies, 1941, p. 491.
2. *Adaptation and Appropriation*, London and New York: Routledge, 2006, p. 27.
3. Foreword to *The Shakespeare Myth*, ed. Graham Holderness, Manchester: Manchester University Press, 1988, p. ix.
4. *Shakespeare Recycled: The Making of Historical Drama*, Hemel Hempstead: Harvester Wheatsheaf, 1992, p. 42.
5. Ibid.
6. 'Introduction', *Shakespeare and Appropriation*, London: Routledge, 1999, pp. 1–14, p. 4.
7. J.M. Barrie, *Peter Pan and Other Plays*, Oxford: Oxford University Press, 1995, p. 75.
8. This can't help remind us of the scene in the novel which describes Peter 'thinning out' the Lost Boys when they grow too big. *Peter Pan*, 1911; rpt. London: Puffin, 1994, p. 72.
9. 'To the Five: A Dedication', in J.M.Barrie, *Peter Pan and Other Plays*, p. 75.

10. George died in action in March 1915 during the First World War; Michael was drowned in Oxford in May 1921. Peter committed suicide in 1960.
11. Quoted in Andrew Birkin, *J.M. Barrie and the Lost Boys: The Real Story Behind Peter Pan*, New Haven, CT: Yale University Press, 2003, p. 196.
12. Ibid., p. 259.
13. Ibid., p. 217.
14. *Peter Pan*, p. 44.
15. Ibid., p. 20.
16. Ibid., p. 72.
17. Henry A. Giroux, 'Memory and Peagogy in the "Wonderful World of Disney"', in *From Mouse to Mermaid: The Politics of Film, Gender and Culture*, ed. Elizabeth Bell, Lynda Haas and Laura Sells Bloomington: Indiana University Press, 1995, p. 46.
18. See Eleanor Byrne and Martin McQuillan, *Deconstructing Disney*, London: Pluto, 1999.
19. *Peter Pan*, p. 242.
20. Ibid., p. 40.
21. In Bell et al., *From Mouse to Mermaid*, p. 196.
22. http://www.eyeweekly.com/eye/issue/issue_12.25.03/film/onscreen.php (accessed 16 July 2007).
23. See note 1 above.
24. Wendy Ide, http://entertainment.timesonline.co.uk/tol/arts_and_entertainment/film/article499627.ece (accessed 10 October 2007).

5   Beyond Fidelity: Transtextual Approaches

1. Some of this material first appeared in D. Cartmell and I. Whelehan, 'Harry Potter and the Fidelity Debate', in *Books in Motion: Adaptation, Intertextuality, Authorship*, ed. Mireia Aragay, Amsterdam and New York: Rodopi, 2005, pp. 37–50.
2. Robert Stam, 'Introduction: The Theory and Practice of Adaptation', in *Literature and Film: A Guide to the Theory and Practice of Film Adaptation*, ed. Robert Stam and Alessandra Raengo, Malden, MA, Oxford and Victoria: Blackwell, 2005, pp. 1–52, p. 27.
3. Ibid., p. 27.
4. See Introduction, p. 7.
5. 'Bewitched, bothered, and bored: Harry Potter, the movie', http://web6.epntet.com/delivery.asp?tb=0CAP7cf+0&print=Print&ad+on&ft=on&est=
6. BBC i Films, 4 November 2001, http://www.bbc.co.uk/films/2001/11/06/harry_potter_philosophers_stone_2001_review.shtml (accessed 3 November 2009).
7. http://www.imdb.com/title/tt0241527/usercomments (accessed 3 November 2009).

8. Anthony Holden, 'Why Harry Potter doesn't cast a spell over me', *Observer Review*, 25 June 2000. http://observer.guardian.co.uk/review/story/0,6903,335923,00.html (accessed 3 November 2009).
   On the whole, the books have been dismissed by a significant number of academic critics as derivative. Jack Zipes, for example, articulates the gap between popular taste and academic scholarship in the concluding chapter of *Sticks and Stones: The Troublesome Success of Children's Literature from Slovenly Peter to Harry Potter*, New York: Routledge, 2001:

   > I am not certain whether one can talk about a split between a minority of professional critics, who have misgivings about the quality of the Harry Potter books and the great majority of readers, old and young, who are mesmerized by the young magician's adventures. But I am certain that the phenomenal aspect of the reception of the Harry Potter books has blurred the focus for anyone who wants to take literature for young people seriously and who may be concerned about standards and taste that adults create for youth culture in the West. (p. 171)

9. Jim Welsh, *Literature/Film Quarterly*, 2002, http://lion.chadwych.co.uk, 2.
10. This list is gathered from I.Q. Hunter (lecture at De Montfort University, Leicester, February 2003) and Pam Cook and Mieke Bernick, *The Cinema Book*, 2nd ed., London: BFI, 1999, pp. 39–42.
11. J.K. Rowling (1997), *Harry Potter and the Philosopher's Stone*, London: Bloomsbury, pp. 70–1.
12. Ibid., p. 90.
13. Ibid., p. 91.
14. Ibid., p. 214.
15. Ibid., p. 209.
16. Peter Krämer, 'Post-Classical Hollywood', in *The Film Studies Reader*, ed. Joanne Hollows, Peter Hutchings and Mark Jancovich, London: Arnold, 2000, pp. 174–80.
17. Nöel King, 'New Hollywood', in *The Cinema Book*, ed. Cook and Bernick, pp. 98–105, p. 103.
18. Richard Keller Simon, *Trash Culture: Popular Culture and the Great Tradition*, Berkeley: University of California Press, 1999, p. 30.
19. *Harry Potter and the Philosopher's Stone*, p. 201. Many thanks to Hester Bradley for drawing our attention to many of these parallels.
20. Ibid., p. 39.
21. Ibid., p. 54.
22. A further similar intertextual reference can be found in the new *Star Trek* film (2009).
23. Suman Gupta, *Re-reading Harry Potter*, Basingstoke: Palgrave Macmillan, 2003, p. 143.
24. Andrew Blake, *The Irresistible Rise of Harry Potter*, London: Verso, 2002, p. 16.

6 Genre and Adaptation: Genre, Hollywood, Shakespeare, Austen

1. *A Natural Perspective: The Development of Shakespearean Comedy and Romance,* New York: Columbia University Press, 1965, p. 1.
2. 2.2. 398–401.
3. *Genre and Hollywood,* London and New York: Routledge, 2000, p. 85.
4. Neale discusses how genre theory came to displace auteurism (*Genre and Hollywood,* London: Routledge, 2000, p. 10). Thomas Schatz, in *Hollywood Genres* (Boston and Madison: McGraw Hill, 1981), sees the auteurist and genre approaches overlapping: 'In fact the *auteur* approach, in asserting a director's consistency of form and expression, effectively translates an auteur into a virtual genre unto himself, into a system of conventions which identify his work' (p. 9).
5. *Film/Genre,* London: BFI, 1999, p. 14.
6. See Thomas Leitch, 'Adaptation, the Genre', *Adaptation,* 1(2), 106–230.
7. We do not wish to enter into the debate as to what does and does not qualify as 'British heritage'; as Claire Monk has indicated, it is a critical construct rather than descriptive of any single film genre. In terms of its constructions, Monk points out that a film does not even need to be British or set in the past in order to be included under the umbrella of 'British heritage': 'The British Heritage-film Debate Revisited', in *British Historical Cinema: The History, Heritage and Costume Film,* London and New York: Routledge, 2002, pp. 17–98)). For a lucid account of the bewildering directions of the debate, see Eckart Voigts-Virchow's introduction to *Janespotting and Beyond: British Heritage Retrovisions since the Mid-1990s,* Tübingen: Gunter Narr, 2004, pp. 9–34.
8. http://www.imdb.com/title/tt0045251/ (accessed 28 November 2005).
9. http://www.imdb.com/title/tt0184791/ (accessed 28 November 2005).
10. http://www.imdb.com/title/tt0119669/ (accessed 28 November 2005).
11. *Shakespeare and Modern Popular Culture,* Oxford: Oxford University Press, 2002, p. 95.
12. Chris Fitter, 'A Tale of Two Branagh's *Henry V,* Ideology and the Mekong Agincourt', in *Shakespeare Left and Right,* ed. Ivo Kamps, London: Routledge, 1991, p. 270.
13. Neale, *Genre and Hollywood,* p. 64.
14. *Popular Fiction: The Logics and Practice of a Literary Field,* London and New York: Routledge, 2004.
15. From *Hollywood Cinema: An Introduction,* Oxford: Blackwell, 1995, p. 107. Quoted in Neale, *Genre and Hollywood,* p. 231.
16. pp. 231–55.
17. *The Times,* 1 January 1936, p. 35.
18. See John Collick, *Shakespeare, Cinema and Society,* Manchester: Manchester University Press, 1999.
19. *Shakespeare on Film,* Harlow: Longman, 2005, p. 142.
20. London: George Allen & Unwin, 1942, p. 25.

21. 'Two conversations with Andrew Davies, in *The Cambridge Companion*, ed. Deborah Cartmell and Imelda Whelehan, pp. 239–51, p. 244.
22. *Film Adaptation & Its Discontents: From 'Gone with the Wind' to The Passion of the Christ*, Baltimore: Johns Hopkins University Press, 2007, pp. 93–126.
23. *Genre in Hollywood*, p. 60.
24. London and New York: Hambledon, 2003.
25. Ibid., p. 116.
26. Richard Burt writes on the ways in which the film dramatises the success of the female writer within a patriarchal society by framing the film with Jane reading, initially to a bored and unimpressed Tom Lefroy (whose criticism, like that of Darcy, Jane overhears), and ending with an enraptured Lefroy listening to the famous Austen giving a rare public reading. The implication is that Jane's achievement is one of changing the male attitude to the female author. *Adaptation* 1(1), 58–62.
27. See Chapter 1, note 6.

7   A Simple Twist? The Genrification of Nineteenth-Century Fiction

1. Armstrong and Miller's series featured a weekly sketch set in a ballroom with a male and female character in period costume dancing with due propriety, but the scene is rapidly undercut by the lewd suggestions they make to each other in exactly the same register, and while dancing.
2. *Literature and Film: A Guide to the Theory and Practice of Film Adaptation*, ed. Robert Stam and Alessandra Raengo, Oxford: Blackwell, 2005, p. 4.
3. 'Adaptation, the Genre', *Adaptation*, 1(2), 2008, 106–20.
4. See McFarlane, *Charles Dickens' 'Great Expectations': The Relationship between Text and* Film, London: Methuen, 2008.
5. Ibid., p. 126.
6. Michael J. Johnson, 'Not Telling the Story the Way It Happened: Alfonso Cuarón's Great Expectations', *Literature/Film Quarterly* 33(1), 2005, 63.
7. *The Mayor of Casterbridge* (1886), ed. and intro. Martin Seymour-Smith, Harmondsworth: Penguin, 1978, p. 411.
8. Ibid., p. 94.
9. A point noted by Gayla S. McGlamery in 'Hardy Goes West: The Claim, The Western, and *The Mayor of Casterbridge*', *Literature/Film Quarterly*, 35(1), 2007, 369–77.
10. George Eliot, *Silas Marner* (1861), ed. Q.D. Leavis, Harmondsworth: Penguin, 1967, p. 164.
11. Review of *A Simple Twist of Fate* by Hal Hinson, 2 September 1994, http://www.washingtonpost.com/wp-srv/style/longterm/movies/videos/asimpletwistoffatepg13hinson_a0a848.htm (accessed 4 August 2008).

12. Stam, in *Literature and Film: A Guide to the Theory and Practice of Film Adaptation*, p. 42.
13. Christine Geraghty, *Now a Major Motion Picture: Film Adaptations of Literature and Drama*, Lanham, MD: Rowman & Littlefield, 2008, p. 16.
14. Ibid., p. 16.
15. Ibid.
16. Steve Neale, *Genre and Hollywood*, London: Routledge, 2000, p. 31.
17. Jane Tompkins, 'West of Everything', in Derek Longhurst, *Gender, Genre and Narrative Pleasure*, London: Unwin Hyman, 1989, p. 29.
18. Stam, *Literature and Film*, p. 46.
19. Thomas Leitch, 'Adaptation, the Genre', *Adaptation*, 1(2), 2008, 107.

8 *Les Liaisons Dangereuses*: Letters on Screen

1. Choderlos de Laclos, *Dangerous Liaisons* (*Les Liaisons Dangereuses*), trans. with an introduction by Helen Constantine, London: Penguin, 2007, p. 185.
2. Ibid., Publisher's Note, p. 3.
3 Ibid., Editor's Preface, p. 6.
4. There have been at least two major television adaptations – *Les Liaisons Dangereuses* (Barma, 1980) and *Les Liaisons Dangereuses* (Dayan, 2003) – but for the purposes of this discussion we will restrict ourselves to film versions.
5. As cited in Roger Ebert's review of the film, published in the *Chicago Sun-Times* on 12 November 1989 (http://rogerebert.suntimes.com/apps/pbcs.dll/article?AID=/19891112/REVIEWS/911120301/1023, accessed 12 November 2009).
6. Quoted in Richard Frohock, 'Adaptation and Cultural Criticism: *Les Liaisons Dangereuses 1960* and *Dangerous Liaisons*', in *The Eighteenth Century on Screen*, ed. Robert Mayer, Cambridge: Cambridge University Press, 2002, p. 161.
7. Carol Hall, 'Valmont Redux: The Fortunes and Filmed Adaptations of *Les Liaisons Dangereuses* by Choderlos de Laclos', *Literature/Film Quarterly*, 19(1), 1991, 44.
8. Gérard Philippe, who played Valmont, was to die later that same year – 1959.
9. Quoted in the introduction to Laclos, *Dangerous Liaisons*, p. xi.
10. Frohock, 'Adaptation and Cultural Criticism: *Les Liaisons Dangereuses 1960 and Dangerous Liaisons*', p. 157.
11. Ibid., p. 165.
12. Ibid., p.168.
13. *Dangerous Liaisons*, p. 187.
14. Kathryn Carson, '*Les Liaisons Dangereuses* on Stage and Film', *Literature/Film Quarterly*, 19(1), 1991, 36.
15. 'Richard Schickel, 'Mean Pills', *Time*, 153(10), 15 March 1999, 84.

16. Ibid., p. 84.
17. Karen Hollinger, 'Losing the Feminist Drift: Adaptations of *Les Liaisons Dangereuses*', *Literature/Film Quarterly*, 24(3), 1996, 293–301, p. 294.
18. Ibid., p. 295.
19. Roz Kaveney, *Teen Dreams: Reading Teen Films and Television*, London: I.B. Tauris, 2006, p. 128.
20. Ibid., p. 135.
21. Timothy Shary, *Teen Movies: American Youth on Screen*, London: Wallflower Press, 2005, p. 90.
22. Brigitte Humbert, 'Cruel Intentions: Adaptation, Teenage Movie or Remake?', *Literature/Film Quarterly*, 30 (4), 2002, 279–86, p. 280.
23. Thomas Doherty, *Teenagers and Teenpics: The Juvenilisation of the American Movies in the 1950s*, rev. Philadelphia: Temple University Press, 2002, p. 1.

Conclusion: Impure Cinema – Another Apology for Adaptations

1. *Adaptation* 1 (1), 2008, 1–4.
2. In *An Age for All Time: The English Renaissance In and Beyond Popular Shakespeare*, ed. Gregory Semenza, Basingstoke: Palgrave Macmillan, forthcoming.
3. Lanham, MD: Rowman and Littlefield, 2008.
4. *The Cambridge Companion to Literature on Screen*, ed. Deborah Cartmell and Imelda Whelehan, Cambridge: Cambridge University Press, 2007, pp. 226–38.
5. *Adaptation* 1(1), 2008, 5–23.
6. See Note 3 above.
7. Baltimore: Johns Hopkins University Press, 2007.
8. Ibid. and London, Routledge, 2006.
9. 'Feminism and Adaptation', conference at De Montfort University, Leicester, 22 April 2009.
10. *Novels into Film*, Berkeley: University of California Press, p. 143.
11. p. 146.
12. John Patterson, *Guardian*, 15 March 2008.
13. Ibid.
14. André Bazin, *What is Cinema?* (trans. Timothy Barnard), Montreal: Caboose, 2009.
15. 'In Defence of Mixed Cinema', in *What Is Cinema?* Vol. 1, trans. Hugh Gray, Berkeley, University of California Press, 1967, pp. 53–75, p. 61.

Bibliography

Allingham, Philip, 'Screening *The Mayor of Casterbridge*', in T.R. Wright (ed.), *Thomas Hardy on Screen*, Cambridge: Cambridge University Press, 2005.

Altman, Rick, *Film/Genre*, London: BFI, 1999.

Andrew, Dudley, 'The Well-worn Muse: Adaptation in Film History and Theory', in Syndy M. Conger and Janice R. Welsch (eds), *Narrative Strategies: Original Essays in Film and Prose Fiction*, Macomb: Western Illinois University Press, 1980, pp. 11–17.

Aragay, Mireia (ed.), *Books in Motion: Adaptation, Intertextuality, Authorship*, Amsterdam and New York: Rodopi, 2005.

Aycock, Wendell and Michael Schoenecke (eds), *Film and Literature: A Comparative Approach to Adaptation*, Lubbock: Texas Tech University Press, 1988.

Balázs, Béla, *Theory of the Film: Character and Growth of a New Art* (trans. from Hungarian by Edith Bone), New York: Dover Publications, 1970 [the first Hungarian edition was in 1948 and this edition is based on the first English translation of 1952].

Barrie, J.M., *Peter Pan* (1911), Harmondsworth: Puffin, 1994.

Barrie, J.M., *Peter Pan and Other Plays*, Oxford: Oxford University Press, 1995.

Barthes, Roland, *Image–Music–Text*, London: Fontana, 1977.

Bazin, André, *What is Cinema?* (ed. and trans) Hugh Gray, Berkeley and London: University of California Press, 1967.

Bazin, André, 'Adaptation, or the Cinema as Digest' in James Naremore (ed.), *Film Adaptation*, London: Athlone, 2000.

Bazin, André, 'In Defense of Mixed Cinema' in *What is Cinema?* (essays trans. and selected by Hugh Gray, forewords by Jean Renoir and Dudley Andrew), Vol. 1, Berkeley: University of California Press, 2005, pp. 53–75.

Bazin, André, *Qu'est-ce que le cinema?*, Paris: Cerf-Corlet, 2008.

Beja, Morris, *Film & Literature: An Introduction*, New York and London: Longman, 1979.

Bell, Elizabeth, Lynda Haas and Laura Sells (eds), *From Mouse to Mermaid: The Politics of Film, Gender and Culture*, Bloomington: Indiana University Press, 1995.

Bignell, Jonathan, *Writing and Cinema*, Harlow: Longman, 1999.

Birkin, Andrew, *J.M. Barrie and the Lost Boys: The Real Story Behind Peter Pan*, New Haven: Yale University Press, 2003.

Blake, Andrew, *The Irresistible Rise of Harry Potter*, London: Verso, 2002.

Bluestone, George, *Novels into Film*, Berkeley: University of California Press, 1957.

Bordwell, David, *Narration in the Fiction Film*, London: Routledge, 1985.

Bordwell, David and Kristin Thompson, *Film Art*, 4th ed., New York and London: McGraw Hill, 1993.

Boyum, Joy Gould, *Double Exposure: Fiction into Film*, New York: New American Library, 1985.

Brannigan, John, *New Historicism and Cultural Materialism*, Basingstoke: Macmillan, 1998.

Brooker-Bowers, Nancy, *The Hollywood Novel and other Novels about Film, 1912–1982*, New York: Garland, 1985.

Buchanan, Judith, *Shakespeare on Film*, Harlow: Longman, 2005.

Burnett, R.G. and E.D. Martell, *The Devil's Camera*, London: Epworth Press, 1932.

Burningham, Bruce R., 'Walt Disney's *Toy Story* as Postmodern *Don Quixote*', *Cervantes: Bulletin of the Cervantes Society of America*, 20(1), 2000, 157–74.

Burt, Richard, 'Becoming literary, becoming historical: the scale of female authorship in *Becoming Jane*', *Adaptation*, 1(1), 2008, 58–62.

Cardwell, Sarah, *Adaptation Revisited: Television and the Classic Novel*, Manchester: Manchester University Press, 2002.

Carson, Kathryn, '*Les Liaisons Dangereuses* on Stage and Film', *Literature/ Film Quarterly*, 19(1), 1991, 35–40.

Cartmell, Deborah, 'Film as the New Shakespeare and Film on Shakespeare: Reversing the Shakespeare/Film Trajectory', *Literature Compass*, 3(5), 2006, 1150–9.

Cartmell, Deborah, I.Q. Hunter, Heidi Kaye and Imelda Whelehan (eds), *Pulping Fictions: Consuming Culture Across the Literature/Media Divide*, London: Pluto, 1996.

Cartmell, Deborah, I.Q. Hunter, Heidi Kaye and Imelda Whelehan (eds), *Trash Aesthetics: Popular Culture and its Audience*, London: Pluto Press, 1997.

Cartmell, Deborah, I.Q. Hunter, Heidi Kaye and Imelda Whelehan (eds), *Sisterhoods Across the Literature/Media Divide*, London: Pluto Press, 1998.

Cartmell, Deborah, I.Q. Hunter, Heidi Kaye and Imelda Whelehan (eds), *Alien Identities*, London: Pluto Press, 1999.

Cartmell, Deborah, I.Q Hunter, Heidi Kaye and Imelda Whelehan (eds), *Classics in Film and Fiction*, London: Pluto Press, 2000.

Cartmell, Deborah, I.Q. Hunter and Imelda Whelehan (eds), *Retrovisions: Reinventing the Past in Film and Fiction*, London: Pluto Press, 2001.

Cartmell, Deborah and Imelda Whelehan (eds), *Adaptations: From Text to Screen, Screen to Text*, London: Routledge, 1999.

Cartmell, Deborah and Imelda Whelehan (eds), *The Cambridge Companion to Literature on Screen*, Cambridge: Cambridge University Press, 2007.

Chatman, Seymour, *Coming to Terms: The Rhetoric of Narrative in Fiction and Film*, Ithaca, New York and London: Cornell University Press, 1990.

Clark, Virginia M., *Aldous Huxley and Film*, Metuchen, NJ and London: Scarecrow Press, 1984.

Clayton, B., 'Shakespeare and the Talkies', *English Review*, 44, 1929, 739–52.

Coats, Paul, *Film at the Intersection of High and Mass Culture*, Cambridge: Cambridge University Press, 1994.

Cohen, Keith, *Film and Fiction: The Dynamics of Exchange*, New Haven: Yale University Press, 1979.

Collick, John, *Shakespeare, Cinema and Society*, Manchester: Manchester University Press, 1989.

Collins, Jim, *High-Pop: Making Culture into Popular Entertainment*, Oxford: Blackwell, 2002.

Conger, Syndy M. and Janice R. Welsch (eds), *Narrative Strategies: Original Essays in Film and Prose Fiction*, Macomb: Western Illinois University Press, 1980.

Cook, Pam and Mieke Bernick, *The Cinema Book* (2nd ed), London: BFI, 1999.

Cook, Pam and Philip Dodd (eds), *Women and Film: A Sight and Sound Reader*, London: Scarlet Press, 1996.

Corrigan, Timothy, *Film and Literature: An Introduction and Reader*, Englewood Cliffs, NJ: Prentice Hall, 2000.

Davy, Charles, *Footnotes to the Film,* London: Lovat Dickson, 1937.

Desmet, Christy and Robert Sawyer (eds), *Shakespeare and Appropriation*, London: Routledge, 1999.

Desmond, John M. and Peter Hawkes, *Adaptation: Studying Film and Literature,* Boston MA and London: McGraw-Hill, 2006.

Doherty, Thomas, *Teenagers and Teenpics: The Juvenilisation of the American Movies in the 1950s* (revised ed), Philadelphia: Temple University Press, 2002.

Donald, James, Anne Friedberg and Laura Marcus (eds), *Close Up: Cinema and Modernism,* London: Cassell, 1998.

Eaton, Walter Richard, 'Class-Consciousness and the Movies', *Atlantic Monthly,* 115, 1915.

Eisenstein, Sergei, 'Dickens Griffiths and the Film Today' (1944), in Jay Leyda (ed.), *Film Form*, London: Dennis Dobson, 1963, pp. 195–256.

Eisenstein, Sergei, *Eisenstein: Writings 1922–1934,* London and Bloomington: BFI and Indiana University Press, 1988.

Eliot, George, *Silas Marner* (1861), ed. with an intro. by Q.D.Leavis, Harmondsworth: Penguin, 1967.

Ellis, John, *Visible Fictions*, London: Routledge, 1982.

Ellis, Kate and E. Ann Kaplan, 'Feminism in Brontë's *Jane Eyre* and its Film Versions', in Barbara Tepa Lupack (ed.), *Nineteenth Century Women at the Movies: Adapting Classic Women's Fiction to Film*, Bowling Green, OH: Bowling Green State University Popular Press, 1999.

Elliott, Kamilla, *Rethinking the Novel/Film Debate*, Cambridge: Cambridge University Press, 2003.

Fitter, Chris, 'A Tale of Two Branaghs: *Henry V*, Ideology and the Mekong Agincourt', in Ivo Kamps (ed.), *Shakespeare Left and Right*, London: Routledge, 1991.

Fitzgerald, F. Scott, *The Last Tycoon* (1941), London and New York: Penguin, 2001.

Fitzsimmons, Linda and Sarah Street (eds), *Moving Performance: British Stage and Screen, 1890s to 1920s*, Trowbridge: Flicks, 2000.

Frohock, Richard, 'Adaptation and Cultural Criticism: *Les Liaisons Dangereuses 1960* and *Dangerous Liaisons*', in Robert Mayer (ed), *The Eighteenth Century on Screen*, Cambridge: Cambridge University Press, 2002.

Frye, Northrop, *A Natural Perspective: The Development of Shakespearean Comedy and Romance*, New York: Columbia University Press, 1965.

Geduld, Harry M., *Authors on Film*, Bloomington and London: Indiana University Press, 1972.

Gelder, Ken, *Popular Fiction: The Logics and Practice of a Literary Field*, London: Routledge, 2004.

Genette, Gérard, *Paratexts: Thresholds of Interpretation*, 1987 (trans. Jane E. Lewin, Foreword by Richard Macksey), Cambridge: Cambridge University Press, 1997.

Geraghty, Christine, *Now a Major Motion Picture: Film Adaptations of Literature and Drama*, Lanham, MD: Rowman & Littlefield, 2008.

Giddings, Robert, K. Selby and C. Wensley. *Screening the Novel: The Theory and Practice of Literary Dramatization*. London: Macmillan, 1990.

Giddings, Robert and Erica Sheen (eds), *The Classic Novel: From Page to Screen*, Manchester: Manchester University Press, 2000.

Gledhill, Christine and Linda Williams (eds), *Reinventing Film Studies*, London: Hodder Arnold, 2000.

Gray, Jonathan, *Watching with* The Simpsons: *Television, Parody, and Intertextuality*, New York: Routledge, 2006.

Greenblatt, Stephen, *Shakespearean Negotiations*, Princeton: Princeton University Press, 1988.

Gupta, Suman, *Re-Reading Harry Potter*, Basingstoke: Palgrave Macmillan, 2003.

Hall, Carol, 'Valmont Redux: The Fortunes and Filmed Adaptation of *Les Liaisons Dangereuses* by Choderlos de Laclos', *Literature/Film Quarterly*, 19(1), 1991, 41–50.

Hardy, Thomas, *The Mayor of Casterbridge* (1886), ed. and intro. Martin Seymour-Smith, Harmondsworth: Penguin, 1978.

Hauser, Arnold, *The Social History of Art. Four: Naturalism, Impressionism, The Film Age* (1951); rpt. London: Routledge & Kegan Paul, 1962.

H.D., *Collected Poems, 1912–1944*, ed. Louis L. Martz, New York: New Directions, 1983.

Hinson, Hal, review of *A Simple Twist of Fate* in the *Washington Post*, 2 September 1994, http://www.washingtonpost.com/wp-srv/style/longterm/movies/videos/asimpletwistoffatepg13hinson_a0a848.htm (accessed 4 August 2008).

Holden, Anthony, 'Why Harry Potter doesn't cast a spell over me', *Observer*, 25 June 2000, http://observer.guardian.co.uk/review/story/0,6903,335923,00.html

Holderness, Graham (ed.), *The Shakespeare Myth*, Manchester: Manchester University Press, 1988.

Holderness, Graham, *Shakespeare Recycled: The Making of Historical Drama*, Hemel Hempstead: Harvester Wheatsheaf, 1992.

Hollinger, Karen, 'Losing the Feminist Drift: Adaptations of *Les Liaisons Dangereuses*', *Literature/Film Quarterly*, 24(3), 1996, 293–301.

Hollows, Joanne, Peter Hutchings and Mark Jancovich (eds), *The Film Studies Reader*, London: Arnold, 2000.

Horton, Andrew and Stuart Y. McDougal (eds), *Play It Again, Sam: Retakes on Remakes*, Berkeley: University of California Press, 1998.

Housel, Rebecca, *From Camera Lens to Critical Lens: A Collection of Best Essays on Film Adaptation*, Newcastle: Cambridge Scholars Press, 2006.

Humbert, Brigitte, 'Cruel Intentions: Adaptation, Teenage Movie or Remake?', *Literature/Film Quarterly*, 30(4), 2002, 279–86.

Hunter, William, 'The Art-Form of Democracy?', *Scrutiny*, 1(1), 1932, 61–5.

Hunter, William, *Scrutiny of Cinema*, London: Wishart & Co., 1932.

Hutcheon, Linda. *A Theory of Adaptation*, London: Routledge, 2006.

Huxley, Aldous, *Brave New World*, 1932; rpt. London: Vintage, 2004.

Johnson, Michael J., 'Not Telling the Story the Way It Happened: Alfonso Cuarón's Great Expectations', *Literature/Film Quarterly*, 33(1), 2005, 62–78.

Jorgens, Jack, *Shakespeare on Film*, Bloomington: Indiana University Press, 1977.

Kaveney, Roz, *Teen Dreams: Reading Teen Films and Television*, London: I.B. Tauris, 2006.

Kennedy, Margaret, *The Mechanized Muse*, London: George Allen & Unwin, 1942.

Kranz, David and Nancy Mellerski (eds) *In/Fidelity: Essays on Film Adaptation*, Newcastle: Cambridge Scholar's Press, 2008.

Laclos, Choderlos de, *Dangerous Liaisons* (*Les Liaisons Dangereuses*) (trans. and intro. Helen Constantine), London: Penguin, 2007.

Leitch, Thomas, 'Twelve Fallacies in Contemporary Adaptation Theory', *Criticism*, 45, 2003, 149–71.

Leitch, Thomas. *Film Adaptation and its Discontents: From 'Gone with the Wind' to 'The Passion of the Christ'*, Baltimore: Johns Hopkins University Press, 2007.

Leitch, Thomas, 'Adaptation: the Genre', *Adaptation*, 1(2), 2008, 106–20.

Lindsay, Vachel, *The Art of the Moving Picture* (1915; rev. 1992) reprinted in Timothy Corrigan, *Film and Literature: An Introduction and Reader*, Englewood Cliffs, NJ: Prentice Hall, 2000.

Lothe, Jakob. *Narrative in Fiction and Film: An Introduction*, Oxford: Oxford University Press, 2000.

Lupack, Barbara Tepa (ed.), *Nineteenth Century Women at the Movies: Adapting Classic Women's Fiction to Film*, Bowling Green, OH: Bowling Green State University Popular Press, 1999.

MacKail, Denis, *The Story of J.M.B.*, London: Peter Davies, 1941.

Maltby, Richard, *From Hollywood Cinema: An Introduction*, Oxford: Blackwell, 1995.

McCabe, Susan, *Cinematic Modernism: Modernist Poetry and Film*, Cambridge: Cambridge University Press, 2005.

McFarlane, Brian, *Novel to Film: An Introduction to the Theory of Adaptation*, Oxford: Oxford University Press, 1996.

McFarlane, Brian, *Charles Dickens' "Great Expectations": A Close Study of the Relationship Between Text and Film*, London: Methuen, 2008.

McGlamery, Gayla S., 'Hardy Goes West: The Claim, The Western, and *The Mayor of Casterbridge*', *Literature/Film Quarterly*, 35(1), 2007, 369–77.

McKernan, Luke, 'A Scene – *King John* – Now Playing at Her Majesty's Theatre', in Linda Fitzsimmons and Sarah Street (eds), *Moving Performance: British Stage and Screen: 1890s to 1920s*, Trowbridge: Flicks, 2000, pp. 56–68.

Miles, Peter, *Cinema, Literature and Society*, London: Croom Helm, 1987.

Monaco, James. *How to Read a Film* (3rd ed.), Oxford: Oxford University Press, 2000.

Murray, Simone, 'Phantom Adaptations: *Eucalyptus*, the adaptation industry and the film that never was', *Adaptation*, 1(1), 2008, 5–23.

Musser, Charles, 'The Devil's Parody: Horace McCoy's Appropriation and Refiguration of Two Hollywood Musicals', in Robert Stam and Alessandra Raengo (eds), *A Companion to Literature and Film*, Oxford: Blackwell, 2004, pp. 227–57.

Naremore, James (ed.), *Film Adaptation*, London: Athlone, 2000.

Neale, Steve, *Genre and Hollywood*, London: Routledge, 2000.

Nicoll, Allardyce, *Film and Theatre*, London: Harrap, 1936.

Orr, J. and C. Nicholson (eds), *Cinema and Fiction: New Modes of Adapting 1959–1990*, Edinburgh: Edinburgh University Press, 1992.

Rascoe, Burton, 'The Motion Pictures An Industry, Not an Art', *Bookman*, 54(3), 1921, 193–9.

Ray, Robert B., 'The Field of "Literature and Film"', in James Naremore (ed.), *Film Adaptation*, London: Athlone, 2000.

Read, Herbert, *A Coat of Many Colours: Occasional Essays*, London: George Routledge & Sons, 1945.

Reynolds, Peter (ed.), *Novel Images: Literature in Performance*, London: Routledge, 1993.

Richardson, Robert D., *Literature and Film*, Bloomington and London: Indiana University Press, 1969.

Ross, Harris, *Film and Literature, Literature as Film*, London: Greenwood, 1987.

Rowling, J.K., *Harry Potter and the Philosopher's Stone*, London: Bloomsbury, 1997.

Sanders, Julie. *Adaptation and Appropriation,* London: Routledge, 2006.

Sartre, Jean-Paul, *What is Literature?* trans. Bernard Frechtman, London: Methuen, 1967.

Schickel, Richard, *The Disney Version,* New York: Avon Books, 1968.

Schickel, Richard, 'Mean Pills', *Time*, 153(10), 15 March 1999, 84.

Seger, Linda, *The Art of Adaptation,* New York: Holt, 1992.

Shakespeare, William, *Hamlet*, ed. Ann Thompson and Neil Taylor, London: Thomson Learning, 2006.

Shary, Timothy, *Teen Movies: American Youth on Screen*, London: Wallflower Press, 2005.

Shaughnessy, Robert, 'Theatricality: Stage, Screen and Nation: *Hamlet* and the Space of History', in *A Concise Companion to Shakespeare on Screen*, ed. Diane E. Henderson, Oxford: Blackwell, 2006, pp. 54–76.

Sherwood, Herbert Francis, 'Democracy and the Movies', *Bookman*, 47 (1918), 235–9.

Simon, Richard Keller, *Trash Culture: Popular Culture and the Great Tradition*, Berkeley: University of California Press, 1999.

Sinyard, Neil. *Filming Literature: the Art of Screen Adaptation*, London: Croom Helm, 1987.

Smith, Grahame, *Dickens and the Dream of Cinema*, Manchester: Manchester University Press, 2003.

Spence, John, *Becoming Jane Austen*, Hambledon: London, 2005.

Spiegel, Alan, *Fiction and the Camera Eye: Visual Consciousness in Film and the Modern Novel*, Charlottesville: University Press of Virginia, 1976.

Stam, Robert, *Literature through Film,* Oxford: Blackwell, 2005.

Stam, Robert and Alessandra Raengo (eds), *A Companion to Literature and Film,* Oxford: Blackwell, 2004.

Stam, Robert and Alessandra Raengo (eds), *Literature and Film: A Guide to the Theory and Practice of Film Adaptation,* Oxford: Blackwell, 2005.

Stem, Seymour, 'The Bankruptcy of Cinema as Art', in William J. Perlman (ed.), *The Movies on Trial: The Views and Opinions of Outstanding Personalities: Screen Entertainment Past and Present*, New York: Macmillan, 1936, pp. 113–40.

Stern, Tiffany, *The Rehearsal from Shakespeare to Sheridan* Oxford: Clarendon, 2000.

Swicord, Robin, 'Under the Skin: Adapting Novels for the Screen', in David Kranz and Nancy Mellerski (eds), *In/Fidelity: Essays on Film Adaptation*, Newcastle: Cambridge Scholars Press, 2008.

Taylor, John Russell (ed.), *Graham Greene on Film: Collected Film Criticism 1935–1940*, New York: Simon & Schuster, 1973.

Tibbetts, John C. and James M. Welsh (eds), *Novels into Film* (1998), New York: Facts on File, 2005.

Tompkins, Jane, 'West of Everything', in Derek Longhurst (ed.), *Gender, Genre and Narrative Pleasure*, London: Unwin Hyman, 1989, pp. 10–30.

Uricchio, W. and R.E. Pearson, *Reframing Culture: The Case of the Vitagraph Quality Films*, Princeton: Princeton University Press, 1993.

Vincendeau, Ginette (ed.), *Film/Heritage/Literature: A Sight and Sound Reader*, London: BFI, 2001.

Voigts-Virchow, Eckart (ed.), *Janespotting and Beyond: British Heritage Retrovisions Since the Mid-1990s*, Tübingen: Gunter Narr, 2004.

Wagner, Geoffrey, *The Novel and the Cinema*, Rutherford, NJ: Fairleigh Dickinson University Press, 1975.

Welsh, Jim, 'Classic Demolition: Why Shakespeare Is Not Exactly "Our Contemporary," or, "Dude, Where's My Hankie?"', *Literature/Film Quarterly*, 20(3), 2002, 223–7.

West, Nathanael, *The Day of the Locust*, New York: Buccaneer Books, 1939.

Woolf, Virginia, 'The Cinema', in *The Captain's Death Bed and Other Essays*, London: Hogarth Press, 1950, pp. 160–71.

Zipes, Jack, *The Troublesome Success of Children's Literature from Slovenly Peter to Harry Potter*, New York: Routledge, 2001.

Select Filmography

Adaptation (2002): Dir. Spike Jonze. Starring Nicholas Cage, Meryl Streep
Amleto (1917): Dir. Eleuterio Rodolfi. Starring Ruggero Ruggeri
Becoming Jane (2007): Dir. Julian Jarrold. Starring Anne Hathaway, James McAvoy
Bleak House (BBC TV 2005): Dir. Justin Chadwick, Susanna White. Starring Gillian Anderson, Denis Lawson
The Claim (2000): Dir. Michael Winterbottom. Starring Peter Mullan, Milla Jovovich
A Cock and Bull Story (2005): Dir. Michael Winterbottom. Starring Steve Coogan and Rob Brydon
Cruel Intentions (1999): Dir. Roger Kumble. Starring Sarah Michelle Gellar, Ryan Philippe
Dangerous Liaisons (1988): Dir. Stephen Frears. Starring Glenn Close, John Malkovich
Finding Neverland (2004): Dir. Marc Forster. Starring Johnny Depp, Kate Winslet
Gamlet (1964): Dir. Grigori Kozintsev. Starring Innokenti Smoktunovsky
Great Expectations (1998): Dir. Alfonso Cuarón. Starring Ethan Hawke, Gwyneth Paltrow
Hamlet (1913): Dir. Hay Plumb. Starring Johnston Forbes-Robertson
Hamlet (1948): Dir. Laurence Oliver. Starring Laurence Olivier
Hamlet (1990): Dir. Franco Zeffirelli. Starring Mel Gibson, Glenn Close
Hamlet (1996): Dir. Kenneth Branagh. Starring Kenneth Branagh
Hamlet (2000): Dir. Michael Almereyda. Starring Ethan Hawke
Hamlet: The Drama of Vengeance (1921): Dir. Svend Gade, Heinz Schall. Starring Asta Nielsen
Harry Potter and the Sorcerer's Stone (2001): Dir. Chris Columbus. Starring Daniel Radcliffe
Hook (1991): Dir. Steven Spielberg. Starring Robin Williams
Les Liaisons Dangereuses (1960). Dir. Roger Vadim. Starring Jeanne Moreau, Gérard Philippe
Little Dorrit. BBC TV (2008): Dir. Adam Smith, Dearbhla Walsh, Diarmuid Lawrence. Starring Matthew Macfadyen
Little Women (1933): Dir. George Cukor. Starring Katharine Hepburn
Little Women (1949): Dir. Mervyn LeRoy. Starring June Allyson
Little Women (1994). Dir. Gillian Armstrong. Starring Winona Ryder
Mansfield Park (1999): Dir. Patricia Rozema. Starring Frances O'Connor

A Midsummer Night's Dream (1935): Dir. William Dieterle, Max Reinhardt. Starring James Cagney, Olivia de Havilland

A Midsummer Night's Dream (1999): Dir. Michael Hoffman. Starring Kevin Kline, Michelle Pfeiffer

Peter Pan (1953): Dir. Clyde Geronimi, Wilfred Jackson, Hamilton Luske (Disney)

Peter Pan (2003): Dir. P.J. Hogan. Starring Jason Isaacs, Jeremy Sumpter

Pride and Prejudice (1940): Dir. Robert Z. Leonard. Starring Greer Garson, Laurence Olivier

Pride and Prejudice (1995). BBC TV: Dir. Simon Langton. Starring Jennifer Ehle, Colin Firth

Pride and Prejudice (2005): Dir. Joe Wright. Starring Keira Knightley, Matthew Macfadyen

Return to Neverland (2002): Dir. Robin Budd (Disney)

Shakespeare in Love (1998): Dir. John Madden. Starring Joseph Fiennes, Gwyneth Paltrow

A Simple Twist of Fate (1994): Dir. Gillies MacKinnon. Starring Steve Martin, Gabriel Byrne

Star Wars (1977): Dir. George Lucas. Starring Mark Hamill, Harrison Ford

Untold Scandal (2003): Dir. Je-yong Lee. Starring Mi-suk Lee, Do-yeon Jeon

Valmont (1989): Dir. Milos Forman. Starring Colin Firth, Annette Bening

William Shakespeare's 'Romeo + Juliet' (1996): Dir. Baz Luhrmann. Starring Leonardo DiCaprio, Claire Danes

Index